Great Walks of Sequoia & Kings Canyon National Parks

Text by Robert Gillmore
Photographs by Eileen Oktavec

Great Walks®

No. 6 in a series of full-color, pocket-size guides to the best walks in the world published by Great Walks Inc. Guides already published: *Great Walks of Acadia National Park & Mount Desert, Great Walks of Southern Arizona, Great Walks of Big Bend National Park, Great Walks of the Great Smokies* and *Great Walks of Yosemite National Park.* For more information on all Great Walks guides send $1 (refundable with your first order) to: Great Walks, PO Box 410, Goffstown, NH 03045.

Copyright © 1994 by Great Walks Inc.
Library of Congress Catalog Card Number: 93-77483
ISBN: 1-879741-06-7

COVER: The Senate Group of giant sequoias on the **Congress Trail** *(Walk No. 23).*

CONTENTS

Walks are listed by region below.

Walks in or near these areas of the parks:

Grant Grove: Nos. 1-2.

Cedar Grove: Nos. 3-13.

Between Grant Grove and the Lodgepole Visitor Center: Nos. 14-19.

Lodgepole Visitor Center: No. 20.

Between the Lodgepole Visitor Center and the Giant Forest: Nos. 21-22.

Giant Forest: Nos. 23-31.
Foothills south of the Giant Forest: Nos. 32-34.
Mineral King: Nos. 35-40.
Southern Sequoia National Park: No. 41.
Bearpaw Meadow: No. 42.

What Are Great Walks?

Great Walks invariably offer beautiful and interesting world-class scenery and excellent views in the most picturesque places on earth.

Great Walks are also shorter and easier than the typical hike or climb. They're usually less than five miles long. They can always be walked in a day or less.* And they're almost always on smooth, firm, dry and, most important, *gently graded* trails. (Long, arduous, sweaty treks up rough, steep, rocky trails are *not* Great Walks!)

*One exception: A three-day back-country excursion where you spend your nights and take your meals at Bearpaw Meadow High Sierra Camp (Walk No. 42).

What Are Great Walks Guides?

Great Walks guides carefully describe and, with beautiful full-color photographs, lavishly illustrate the world's Great Walks.

Unlike many walking guides, which describe *every* trail in a region, Great Walks describe only the *best* walks, the happy few that will especially delight you with their beauty.

Unlike many guides, which give you mainly directions, Great Walks guides carefully describe *all* the major features of every Great Walk so you can know, in advance, precisely what the Walk has to offer and exactly *why* it's worth your time to take it.

After all, your leisure time is valuable. In your lifetime you can walk on only a fraction of the hundreds of thousands of miles of trails in the world. Why not walk only the best?

For your convenience Great Walks guides are an easy-to-use and easy-to-carry pocket size and their covers are film laminated for extra protection against wear and tear.

Acknowledgments

We are grateful for the assistance of Jan Blackshire, Tom Burgess, Mary Anne Carlton, Malinee Crapsey, Hannah Merrill, John Satnat and Jim Warner of the National Park Service, Chris Boyer of the US Forest Service, Tyler Conrad of the Sequoia Natural History Association and Melanie Barvitsky and Ramona Goodge of Guest Services, Inc.

Introduction: The Treasures of Sequoia/ Kings Canyon — and How to Enjoy Them

Sequoia and Kings Canyon are separate national parks. But that fact is merely technical. For the twin parks lie side by side, like two pieces of a jigsaw puzzle, along the more-than-two-mile-high crest of the Sierra Nevada. The National Park Service administers them as one park, they're usually toured as one park — a single highway runs through them — and both parks have similar natural features. No wonder they're referred to by a compound name: Sequoia and Kings Canyon.

The name is fortuitous: By calling the combined parks Sequoia and Kings Canyon we identify their two greatest natural treasures: large groves of giant sequoia trees — the world's largest living things — and long, dramatic water- and glacier-carved canyons that are among the deepest in the world.

You can see the parks' world-renowned sequoias and canyons, as well as the bare rock peaks rising above them, on 42 Great Walks. Virtually all the Walks provide views of mountains and canyons and the few that don't take you into dense groves of giant sequoias. In all, 11 Walks — Nos. 1, 14, 18, 23-27, 29, 35 and 42 — offer close views of sequoias. Four Walks — Nos. 7, 11, 20 and 38 — take you to major, named waterfalls and 11 others — Nos. 4, 5, 31-34,

36 and 39-42—take you to smaller, unnamed but still lovely falls and cascades. Four Walks—Nos. 8, 30, 32, 34—feature such Indian artifacts as bedrock mortars and pictographs. Two—Nos. 3 and 31—include tours of marble caves and four others—Nos. 32-34 and 41—take you over the pretty, dry, oak- and grass-covered foothills in the south of Sequoia National Park.

None of these Walks is especially difficult. In fact, 17 of them—Nos. 1, 2, 6-9, 12, 14, 17, 18, 23-26, 34, 37 and 38—are easy or very easy and ten others—Nos. 3, 5, 10, 15 and 27-32—while not quite easy, are nevertheless undemanding. Eight Walks—Nos. 4, 13, 16, 19, 20, 36, 39 and 41—are moderate and only six—Nos. 11, 21, 22, 35, 40 and 42—are moderately strenuous. Walk No. 33 is either moderate or moderately strenuous, depending on whether you drive or walk to the trailhead.

Virtually all the Walks are on smooth, gently graded trails. The *average* walk is only two or three miles long and takes less than half a day to complete. All but one can easily be completed in a day; the exception is Walk No. 42, a three-day excursion where you spend two nights and eat dinner and breakfast at Bearpaw Meadow High Sierra Camp.

If you want to know how long each Walk takes to complete, a very rough rule of thumb is: one hour per mile. Of course, if you walk faster and don't pause to enjoy the views, the time per mile is less.

Depending on your speed, it takes about three weeks to drive to and walk all 42 Great Walks.

If you have time to take just a few of the Walks, we recommend the following, which are all easy or undemanding and relatively short: Moro Rock in the Giant Forest (No. 28) is a world-class walk — perhaps the best in the parks — and shouldn't be missed. The most impressive sequoias in the Giant Forest are on the Congress Trail (Walk No. 23). Nearby, Walk No. 29 (Crescent Meadow) also features many mature sequoias, as well as several wildflower-filled meadows and historic cabins. The General Grant Tree Trail (Walk No. 1), in Grant Grove, has more giant sequoias per foot than any other Walk in the parks. If you're in Grant Grove, also take the short, easy Walk to Panoramic Point (Walk No. 2). If you're traveling between Grant Grove and Giant Forest, stop at Lost Grove (Walk No. 18), a small but dense stand of sequoias. If you're in the foothills, in the southern part of the parks, some or all of Walk No. 32 (Hospital Rock & Paradise Creek) provides a lot to see in a little time, including Indian artifacts and views of the rockbound Middle Fork of the Kaweah River and the Middle Fork canyon. Farther south, Walk No. 34 (Potwisha) offers more Indian artifacts and more views of the Middle Fork. If you go to Cedar Grove you'll enjoy a dramatic, world-class drive into Kings Canyon and you'll be near five quick and easy Walks — Nos. 6-9 and 12 — as well as the dramatic trail along the Windy Cliffs (Walk No. 3).

If you have more time, take these longer Walks, which all have dramatic mountain and canyon views: Mist Falls (Walk No. 11), in Cedar Grove; Big Baldy and Little Baldy (Walks No. 16 and 19), between Grant Grove and Giant Forest; Tokopah Falls, the Watchtower and Panther Gap (Walks No. 20-22), near Giant Forest; the Ladybug Trail (Walk

No. 41), in the southern foothills; and, of course, the three-day trip to Bearpaw Meadow High Sierra Camp (Walk No. 42), east of the Giant Forest. If you have time for the drive to Mineral King (a three-hour round trip from Three Rivers), take the area's two easy Walks (Nos. 37 and 38) and the longer Farewell Gap and White Chief trails (Walks No. 39 and 40).

What's the very best time of year to take these Walks? For most of them — which are in cool evergreen forests above 5,000 feet — the best time is late spring. That's when the trails are clear of snow, when all the roads, caves (see Walks No. 3 and 31) and accommodations in the parks are open and when waterfalls and cascades (which are fed by melting snow) are fullest. The park is also cooler and less crowded in the spring than it is in the summer. On the other hand, Walk No. 42 — a three-day excursion to Bearpaw Meadow High Sierra Camp — can be taken only when the camp is open — usually from mid-June to mid-September. At the other extreme, Walks in the foothills (Nos. 32-34 and 41) may be taken both earlier and later than high-country Walks because temperatures there are warmer and snowfall is rare. Walks No. 3-13 and 35-40 can't be taken in winter because the Kings Canyon Highway and the Mineral King Road are closed because of snow and Walk No. 21 can't be taken in winter because part of the trail is closed. Also, Walks No. 14-19 are inaccessible when the Generals Highway between Grant Grove and Lodgepole Village is closed temporarily because of snow.

Here is some more information as well as a few suggestions to help you get the most out of these Great Walks:

►This guide tells you *exactly* what each Walk has to offer. Take advantage of it by reading it before you take *any* Walks. That way you'll be best able to select Walks that most closely suit your taste.

►Carry the guide on all Walks. (It'll fit easily in any pocket.) It tells you how to reach the trailhead and gives you exact directions for each Walk, as well as detailed descriptions of what you'll see.

►Follow our directions. The Walks start where they start, stop where they stop and go where they go for two reasons: (1) the routes we describe provide the best walking in the parks; (2) any other trails are more difficult, less scenic or both.

►Nearly all trailheads and trail junctions are well marked, almost every trail is easy to follow and in any event we tell you everything you need to know to find your way. If, however, you like to follow a map or want to use one to help identify the parks' natural landmarks, here are six recommendations: The parks' *Official Map and Guide,* like all similar National Park Service publications, clearly and attractively indicates all roads in and near the park, as well as major trails, creeks, mountains and other natural and manmade features. It's yours for free at all park entrance stations. Also very helpful are large-scale maps of the Cedar Grove, Giant Forest, Mineral King and Lodgepole/Wolverton areas published by the Sequoia Natural History Association, and the topographical *Recreation Map of Sequoia & Kings Canyon National Parks* published by Tom Harrison. All are sold, at modest prices, in visitor centers and stores throughout the parks.

►Another publication you might want to buy is

Exploring Mountain Highways: A Road Guide to Sequoia and Kings Canyon National Parks, published by the Sequoia Natural History Association. It's an eloquent, detailed description of what you see from the parks' major roads. The best guide to park accommodations is the *Sequoia & Kings Canyon National Parks Magazine,* which is available without charge from the park concessioner, Guest Services, at PO Box 789, Three Rivers CA 93271; 209-561-3314. The handsome, colorful magazine also touches on the park's history and scenic attractions. Schedules of activities are listed in the parks' free newspaper, *Sequoia Bark,* available at all entrance stations.

►Unless you're in excellent condition (and few people are) do your body a favor: Whenever possible, do the Walks in order of difficulty, easiest ones first. That way each Walk will help prepare you to take the harder one that follows. Ideally, you'll be able to progress from short, easy Walks to long, moderately strenuous ones—such as the Walk to Bearpaw Meadow High Sierra Camp (No. 42)—without much difficulty.

►Begin each Walk early enough so you can finish it comfortably before dark.

►On longer walks, carry a small flashlight in case you can't get back before dark, as well as some toilet paper and Band-Aids.

►Any comfortable walking shoes are fine for short Walks that follow smooth paths (Nos. 1, 2, 6, 7, 9, 12, 17, 25, 26, 28, 31 and 34, for example). For other Walks we recommend the greater support and protection provided by above-the-ankle hiking boots. To avoid unnecessary discomfort (or even blisters) make sure your footwear fits and is broken in before you start walking.

►Ordinarily, summer weather in the Sierra is excellent for walking. It's fair and comfortable and rain is rare. (Most of the precipitation in the parks is winter snow.) But it does rain occasionally. To stay dry (and avoid possible hypothermia) we suggest you carry rain gear and wear waterproof hiking boots on cloudy days and especially on longer Walks. For best protection, we recommend a waterproof hooded jacket and pants. The most comfortable rain garments are "breathable," which means they keep rain out but also let perspiration escape.

►Remember that the weather gets cooler as the altitude gets higher. If your excursion involves a big gain in elevation, bring along a sweater, jacket or windbreaker.

►Carry water on longer Walks. It will taste best if you carry it in ceramic canteens, such as the French-made Tournus, rather than plastic or metal bottles. If you have access to a refrigerator, here's a way to keep water cold: The night before a Walk pour a couple of inches in the canteen and lay it on its side in the freezer, leaving the top open to make sure the canteen doesn't crack when the water freezes and expands. Next morning fill the canteen with cold water. The ice already inside will keep the water cold.

►Never drink water from any stream or spring without either boiling it, filtering it or treating it with purifying tablets. The risk of an attack of *giardia lamblia* is too great to drink untreated water.

►Never urinate or defecate within 100 feet of

creeks or lakes and don't wash yourself or your dishes in them. (Even biodegradable soap will pollute a lake or stream if used directly in them.)

▶It's obvious but it bears repeating: Binoculars enable you to see what you can't see without them. A high-powered, light-weight pair is worth carrying.

▶Use enough sun screen to keep the exposed parts of your body from burning and wear something to keep the sun out of your eyes. We favor a wide-brimmed hat or a sun visor over tinted sunglasses, which substitute a tinted view of the world for the real one. Also, a hat or visor helps keep you cool by protecting much of your face from the sun.

▶Mosquitoes and other flying insects can sometimes be a pesty problem on Walks near marshes, such as Nos. 8-12, in the Cedar Grove area, and the first part of the Ladybug Trail (Walk No. 41). Carry some repellent, just in case.

▶Ticks carrying Lyme disease are found in the foothills of Sequoia National Park. On Walk Nos. 31-34 and 41 try to avoid contact with brush (which can harbor ticks) by wearing long pants and staying on the trail. Also check your skin periodically and carefully remove any ticks with tweezers. Rattlesnakes are also seen occasionally in the foothills — another good reason for staying on the trail and for putting your feet or hands only where you can see them.

▶Some park trails, particularly those on longer Walks, are used by horses and mules. To avoid startling them, move off the trail and stand still when they go by.

▶You'll probably see black bears. Don't worry

about them. Unlike grizzly bears (which don't live in California) black bears don't attack people—unless they think they're threatening their cubs. So if you see a bear, keep your distance, look for cubs (they may be in a tree) and make sure you don't come between them and their mother.

►Don't feed *any* wild animals. If bears become accustomed to human food and to the places where it's found, they become nuisances (by breaking into cars, etc.) and often have to be destroyed. The moral: If you really want to be nice to animals, admire them from a distance but let them find their own dinner. Also, don't leave any food or garbage where wild animals can get it. Dump your trash in refuse barrels, not along the trail.

►Poison oak is found along some trails, particularly those in sunny spots below 5,000 feet. Learn to recognize it—its small lobed leaves (like miniature oak leaves) grow in groups of three. To make sure you don't walk through it, stay on the trail.

►Be careful when swimming in the parks' rivers. The water is cold and the current is often swift, especially in the spring.

►Climbing up waterfalls or down cliffs is dangerous. The National Park Service warns you not to do it, and so do we.

►Walk only on established trails.

►We carefully describe the falls, cascades and other water features you'll see on these Walks. Keep in mind, however, that they may look different in unusually wet or dry weather and that they're usually fuller in the spring than in the fall.

►Remember that the world's only constant is

change. The locations of the mountains on these Walks won't vary from year to year but anything subject to human control—trail routes, parking lots, signs and so on—can change. Be alert for trail re-routings and follow signs.

►Above all, remember that a Great Walk is mainly an aesthetic activity, not an athletic one. Its primary purpose is not to give you exercise (although exercise you will surely get) but to show you exceptional natural beauty. Walk slowly enough to savor it. Most people walk too fast. Don't make their mistake. You no more want to rush through these Walks than you want to rush through the Louvre.

How to Get There, Where to Stay, Where to Eat

The Walks are found in every section of the parks that can be reached by road. Four Walks are technically just outside the parks, in the Sequoia National Forest.

* * *

Walks No. 1 and 2 are in the Grant Grove area of Kings Canyon National Park. Grant Grove is 50 miles east of Fresno, via Route 180. It's also at the northern end of the Generals Highway, which links Grant Grove with the Sequoia National Park entrance at Ash Mountain, about 50 miles away; and it's at the southern end of the Kings Canyon Highway, which connects Grant Grove to Cedar Grove (see below). Services in Grant Grove include a visitor center with interesting exhibits; a gas station; a gift shop; a cocktail lounge; a market; a restaurant serving basic breakfasts, lunches and dinners; two picnic areas; three campgrounds; 43 "rustic" cabins (without electricity or running water) that are heated by wood stoves, lit by kerosene lamps and serviced by a central restroom and showers; and nine rather charming cabins that have electric heat and lights, (real) paneled walls, double casement windows, wooden screens and white-painted bathrooms with hot and cold running water and old-fashioned clawfoot bathtubs.

* * *

Walks No. 3-13 are in or near the Cedar Grove area of Kings Canyon National Park. To get there, you take one of the most dramatic drives in the world, the 38-mile Kings Canyon Highway, which runs from Grant Grove and ends in Kings Canyon 5.5 miles east of Cedar Grove Village.

The well-paved, two-lane highway runs north from Grant Grove through an impressive evergreen forest of incense-cedars, firs, pines and, of course, sequoias. About a mile from the visitor center the road enters Sequoia National Forest and in another mile comes to an overlook, on the left side of the road, from which you can see across the national forest, all the way to the San Joaquin Valley, in the west.

Then the highway begins its long descent into Kings Canyon, the deep chasm along the South Fork of the Kings River. About ten miles from Grant

Grove, the road drops into the drier upper foothills of the Sierra. Here the evergreen trees are gradually replaced by scrub oaks, yuccas, grasses and other low-growing plants that need much less moisture than conifers. Here too you'll get your first glimpses of both the South Fork and Middle Fork canyons, the bottoms of which are more than half a mile below you.

As the road switches back and forth down the steep walls of the South Fork canyon, you'll have continuous open views of both the South and Middle Fork canyons and the two-mile-high peaks beyond them. The steep, creased landscape before you is bare of trees; without them you can see the very bones of the earth.

About 14 miles from Grant Grove you reach Junction View, an overlook on the left side of the road from which you can see the intersection, or junction, of the South and Middle forks of the Kings River, 2,500 feet below you. A plaque here notes that the highest peak on the north wall of the canyon— 10,051-foot Spanish Mountain—is more than 7,800 feet above the bottom of the canyon. That makes this gorge the deepest in North America. (The Grand Canyon is only about 5,400 feet deep.) The plaque also identifies some of the 2.5-mile-high Sierra peaks to the north. Look to your right and you'll see upper Kings Canyon. That's where you'll be in a few minutes.

In another two miles you'll cross Ten-Mile Creek, which flows into the Kings River, and a mile later you'll be on the inner gorge of the South Fork Canyon. The highway now winds along a shelf carved into the clifflike walls of the chasm.

About 21 miles from Grant Grove the road twists back and forth through perhaps the most dramatic part of the drive: Horseshoe Bend. Here the vertical rock walls of the canyon are just a few hundred feet apart and the river is almost directly below you, in the bottom of a deep, steep gorge. You'll have to lean forward to see the tops of the canyon walls through your windshield.

Finally you come to the edge of the river, near the entrance to Boyden Cavern (Walk No. 3). You're now about 22 miles from, and 3,500 feet lower than, Grant Grove.

The road immediately crosses the South Fork, passes below the Windy Cliffs (Walk No. 3), on the south side of the canyon, and closely follows the cascading river upstream.

About 5.5 miles from Boyden Cavern you'll come to the Grizzly Falls parking area, on the left side of the road. The falls, which cascade over a 30-foot-high granite ledge, are just a few hundred feet from the highway.

Less than three miles from the falls you'll leave the Sequoia National Forest and enter the Cedar Grove section of Kings Canyon National Park. Here the shape of Kings Canyon starts to change. West of Cedar Grove the canyon is a narrow, V-shaped valley whose walls rise directly from the river. This part of the canyon has been carved by the river, which cuts deeper and deeper into the canyon as it washes away the ground beneath it. In Cedar Grove, the canyon is U-shaped, with nearly vertical walls and a wide, flat valley floor. Like Yosemite Valley, the canyon in Cedar Grove was carved by glaciers—

huge, slow-moving rivers of snow and ice, hundreds of feet high and hundreds of feet wide.

Not surprisingly, Kings Canyon in Cedar Grove shares some characteristics with Yosemite Valley, including smooth, glacier-polished cliff walls, an often placid river that meanders gently over a nearly level valley floor, and a lush forest of incense-cedars, pines and other evergreens growing in the well-watered canyon bottom.

Less than two miles from the park boundary you'll come to the turnoff to Cedar Grove Village, on the left of the road. The biggest building in the village is a large green-stained, rustic-looking wooden structure on the banks of the South Fork. It houses a snack bar and a combination gift shop and grocery store on the first floor and 18 attractive motel rooms on the second. Each room has wall-to-wall carpeting, two queen-size beds, an air-conditioner and a modern three-quarter bath (shower but no tub). The snack bar serves basic but tasty breakfasts, lunches and dinners. And informality is the rule: If you don't want to eat in the snack bar you can take your tray up to your room, to one of two covered porches or — the best idea — to one of several picnic tables beside the South Fork. Also in the village are a gas station, a laundromat, a ranger station and four campgrounds.

Walk No. 4 begins just north of Cedar Grove Village. All the other Walks in Cedar Grove begin along the Kings Canyon Highway between Cedar Grove Village and the end of the road, 5.5 miles farther up the canyon. On your drive to these Walks you'll enjoy many views of the canyon's nearly vertical half-mile-high rock walls. One of the best vistas is from Canyon View, a turnoff on the left side of the road, less than a mile up the canyon from the road to Cedar Grove Village.

* * *

Walks No. 14-20 all begin on or near the Generals Highway between Grant Grove and the Lodgepole Visitor Center, which is just north of Giant Forest Village, in Sequoia National Park. This section of the highway offers many views of evergreen forests, mountains and canyons.

About 4.9 miles south of Grant Grove (and about four miles south of the intersection of the Generals Highway and Route 180) you come to the Redwood Canyon Overlook, on the right (south) side of the road. From here you can see the Redwood Mountain Grove (Walk No. 14), the largest sequoia grove in the world.

About 1.8 miles south of the Redwood Canyon Overlook (and just north of the trail to Buena Vista Peak [Walk No. 15]) is the Kings Canyon Overlook, on the left (north) side of the highway. From here you can see across the Sequoia National Forest and deep into Kings Canyon National Park. A plaque identifies the peaks and the canyons in the distance. Buck Rock (Walk No. 17) is less than three miles away, on the right.

About halfway between Grant Grove and the Lodgepole Visitor Center is Stony Creek Village, which has a gas station, a laundromat, a combination gift shop and market, a restaurant serving breakfast, lunch and dinner, and 11 motel rooms, each with wall-to-wall carpeting and a three-quarter bath. Stony Creek Campground is nearby and Dorst

Campground is about five miles to the south, on the Generals Highway.

Between Little Baldy Saddle (where Walk No. 19 begins) and Lodgepole Village, you'll have frequent views, on the right (south) side of the road, of the foothills of Sequoia National Park and the San Joaquin Valley beyond.

The Lodgepole Visitor Center, which is about 26 miles southeast of Grant Grove, offers interesting exhibits on the history of the parks. Next to the visitor center is a large building housing a laundromat, a gift shop, an ice-cream shop, a delicatessen and the largest grocery store in the parks. A gas station and the Lodgepole Campground are nearby.

* * *

Walks No. 21-31 all begin in or near the Giant Forest, which is just south of the Lodgepole Visitor Center. The Giant Forest—so named by the famed conservationist John Muir—is one of the largest sequoia groves in the world. Here too are the most extensive accommodations in the parks. There are 83 motel rooms, each with wall-to-wall carpeting, two beds and a private bath. There are 96 "rustic" cabins without bathrooms—guests use a central restroom and showers—and some of these have no electricity; they're lit by kerosene lamps. There are also 64 cabins with both private baths and electricity; one is a large "honeymoon" cabin with a fieldstone fireplace. Most of the cabins have one room and two beds but a few have two rooms and as many as four beds. Next to the honeymoon cabin, the most charming accommodations in the Giant Forest—or, for that matter, in both parks — are the *older* "standard" cabins. Rather like the cabins with baths in Grant Grove, these eye-pleasing frame structures have real paneled walls and ceilings, double casement windows and wooden screens, dark-painted wood floors and white-painted bathrooms with old-fashioned clawfoot bathtubs and white-painted wooden stools.

Also in Giant Forest are two gift shops, a lounge, a small market, a cafeteria that serves breakfast, lunch and dinner, and the Giant Forest Lodge Dining Room, which is the best restaurant in the parks. It serves well-prepared breakfasts, dinners and Sunday brunches, its tables are covered with white cloths, the servers are dressed in white shirts and black ties, the salad and dessert bar (with dinner) is sumptuous and giant sequoias are just on the other side of the restaurant's huge windows.

In fact, *all* the facilities in the Giant Forest are nestled beneath sequoias that are almost as wide as the cabins. When you stay in the Giant Forest, you don't merely *visit* the sequoias for a few hours, as other tourists do. You *live* with them. You walk among them when you go to dinner and when you return to your cabin. You sleep beside them at night and you see them when you get up in the morning.

Unfortunately, while this proximity might be pleasant for people, it does no good for the sequoias. That's why the Park Service is building new accommodations in Waksachi, near the Lodgepole Visitor Center — well away from the big trees — and why it plans to dismantle virtually all the buildings in the Giant Forest when the new facilities are ready. So if you want to stay in a picturesque older cabin just a few feet from a sequoia, you'd better do it soon.

* * *

Walks No. 32-34 begin on or near the Generals Highway between Hospital Rock and Potwisha Campground, in the foothills of Sequoia National Park. From Giant Forest Village, the highway immediately begins its winding 17-mile, 4,900-foot descent to the entrance of Sequoia National Park at Ash Mountain.

About 1.7 miles from Giant Forest Village the road passes through an elegant row of four giant sequoias known as the Four Guardsmen.

In another .5 miles the road makes a hairpin turn to the left. This switchback is known as Commissary Curve, after an army commissary that stood here in the early 20th century, when cavalry still guarded the park. The road to Crystal Cave (Walk No. 31) leaves the highway on the right.

One mile farther, on the right side of the road, is Eleven Range Overlook, where you have a wide view across the foothills to the west. You're 5,200 feet high here and at the northern edge of the upper foothills. The foothills get much less rain and snow than the Giant Forest, so as the road descends to the bottom of the Middle Fork canyon the evergreen trees are replaced by oaks and bay laurels, which need much less water than sequoias and firs.

In another mile you'll come to another overlook, from which you can see Deer Ridge and Deep Canyon beyond it.

About 1.6 miles farther you'll reach one of the most dramatic overlooks on the Generals Highway:

Amphitheater Point. From here you can see Moro Rock (Walk No. 28) at the edge of the Giant Forest, more than 2,000 feet above you. In the east you can see the bare gray peaks of the Great Western Divide. (There's a public telephone here too.)

The road keeps twisting back and forth down the steep and increasingly open, grassy slope of the canyon until, almost five miles from Amphitheater Point, you come to Hospital Rock. Walks No. 32 and 33 begin at this interesting place, which is described on pages 147-150. Picnic tables, restrooms and a telephone are beside the parking area on the right (west) side of the road.

By now you've descended to about 2,700 feet. This altitude gets even less precipitation than the area you just drove through, so the oaks and bay laurels have been replaced by manzanita, yucca, wild oats and other drought-resistant flora. Across the low chaparral you'll have many views of the Middle Fork canyon, the Great Western Divide and Castle Rocks, on the canyon's south slope.

About 2.3 miles from Hospital Rock you come to the Potwisha Campground. Walk No. 34 begins nearby.

Other than Potwisha Campground and the Buckeye Flat Campground, east of Hospital Rock, there are no accommodations near Walks No. 32-34. The closest ones are in and around Three Rivers, just south of the park. There you'll find three campgrounds, a dozen motels and a half-dozen restaurants, all between six and 13 miles away from Walks No. 32-34. The Park Service publishes a list of the motels and campgrounds and their phone numbers;

if you want a copy call 209-565-3134. None of the accommodations in Three Rivers, of course, can match the unparalleled natural ambience of the facilities in the Giant Forest, which is about 11 miles from Hospital Rock and about 13 miles from Potwisha.

* * *

Walks Nos. 35-40 begin in or near Mineral King. The trailheads are all at or near the eastern end of the narrow, winding, 25-mile Mineral King Highway. The western end of the highway runs into Route 198 about two miles south of the Ash Mountain entrance of Sequoia National Park and about five miles north of Three Rivers.

To reach the Mineral King Highway from points in Sequoia National Park, take the Generals Highway all the way to the Ash Mountain entrance, which is about four miles from Potwisha Campground. About 1.5 miles from the campground the highway passes under a large granite boulder known as Tunnel Rock. About 1.6 miles later you reach the Ash Mountain Visitor Center, which has restrooms, a telephone and exhibits on the parks. In another .7 miles you'll reach the park entrance and Route 198. Two miles ahead, on the left, is the road to Mineral King.

The only services in Mineral King (or, for that matter, along the entire Mineral King Highway) are two campgrounds and the Silver City Resort. Just four miles from Mineral King, the Silver City Resort includes 11 rustic cabins and a three-bedroom chalet; a small general store that sells a few basic food items, and a restaurant that serves breakfast, lunch and dinner Thursday through Monday, but only snacks (homemade pie, coffee, etc.) on Tuesday and Wednesday. (This schedule may change. Call the resort to ensure you have the latest information.) Like the rustic cabins at Grant Grove and the Giant Forest, none of the cabins at Silver City has electricity. All, however, are furnished with kerosene lanterns, a wood stove or gas heater, kitchen sinks (with cold running water), and bedding and towels. Nine of the cabins are housekeeping units furnished with a gas cooking stove, a barbecue, cooking utensils and dishes; six housekeeping cabins also have refrigerators but only one has a bathroom. The chalet also has a bath, as well as a fully equipped kitchen. Cabins without baths are serviced by central restrooms and showers. You can call the resort at 209-561-3223 when they're open — from late May to early October — and at 209-734-4109 when they're not. Make reservations as early as you can.

It takes about three days to drive to and from Mineral King and to do the area's six Walks. Unless you plan to eat all your meals at the Silver City restaurant, you'll need to buy groceries and cook at a campground or the Silver City Resort. The largest grocery store in or around the parks is in Three Rivers. We suggest you shop there before heading for Mineral King.

From Route 198, the Mineral King Highway immediately winds up the steep, grassy slope of Red Hill. Here you'll see Hanging and Moro rocks (Walk Nos. 27 and 28) and Alta Peak, both to the north, in Sequoia National Park.

About two miles from Route 198 the road climbs

over Red Hill and enters the canyon of the East Fork of the Kaweah River. You can't see the river yet — it's almost 1,000 feet below you, in the bottom of the steep granite gorge on your left. But you'll soon be able to see a long wooden trestle, with a chute on top of it, up the slope on your right. That's the Kaweah Number One flume. It was built in the 1890s to carry water from the East Fork to a hydroelectric plant near Three Rivers and it's still used today.

About 6.5 miles from Route 198 you'll cross the East Fork on a striking concrete arched bridge over a deep, narrow gorge. Then the highway winds up the steep chaparral-covered north slope of the canyon. Here, in the dry foothills of the Sierra, there are no trees to block your view, so you have uninterrupted vistas far up and down the deep canyon.

About nine miles from Route 198 you'll enter Sequoia National Park and a mile later you'll come to Lookout Point Ranger Station. Here you'll have a long view over the foothills on your right.

In another three miles you'll have climbed to about 4,500 feet. This elevation gets more snow and rain than the lower foothills and you'll start to see oaks and bay laurels, which need more moisture than manzanita, chamise and other chaparral vegetation.

About 15 miles from Route 180, you'll have climbed to more than 5,000 feet, an elevation that gets even more precipitation than the upper foothills you just drove through, and you'll start seeing pines and other water-loving evergreens.

About a mile ahead you'll come to Redwood Creek. Here you're about 5,700 feet high, the wettest elevation you've driven through so far on the highway, and the evergreen trees are large and thick enough to block your views of the canyon. Here, too, you'll see your first giant sequoias, on the left side of the road.

Three miles farther you'll come to the Atwell Mill Campground, where Walks No. 35 and 36 begin and where you'll see many more sequoias along the road.

In another mile or so you'll come to Cabin Cove, named for the small, privately owned summer residences built along the highway. What are private houses doing in a national park? This section of the park was part of the Sequoia National Forest until 1978 and the Forest Service leased sites on which people could build cabins. When the area was acquired by the park in 1978, the National Park Service agreed to honor the leases for as long as the leaseholder lived. Eventually these and other private cabins in Mineral King will disappear.

A half-mile ahead is the privately owned enclave known as Silver City. It was named during the heady days of the late 1880s when prospectors hoped to find millions of dollars' worth of silver in Mineral King. Today Silver City consists of summer vacation cabins and the Silver City Resort.

In another mile, the Mineral King Highway crosses a steep slope above the East Fork. Here avalanches have ripped trees away from the hillside. Through the opening in the forest you can see the East Fork, below you on the right, and peaks of the Great Western Divide above Mineral King valley.

About 1.2 miles ahead you'll come to another group of private cabins. This area is known as Faculty Flat because many of the original leaseholders were academics from Los Angeles.

In another .3 miles you'll come to Cold Spring Campground, where Walk No. 37 begins. Then you'll pass the Mineral King Ranger Station, where you'll find interesting exhibits of Mineral King mining history.

Finally, a mile after the ranger station, and more than 24 miles from Route 198, you'll be in the northern end of Mineral King valley, where Walks No. 38-40 all begin. Unlike the heavily forested canyon slopes that you just drove through, Mineral King valley is nearly treeless — the sides of the valley are so steep that avalanches periodically strip off most of the trees that try to grow on them. With only grasses and bushes growing on its walls, Mineral King actually looks like an alpine valley and a bit like the treeless chaparral near Three Rivers, which is 6,000 feet lower. Without trees in your way you have uninterrupted views up and down the long, narrow valley. You can see all the way from the flat bottom of the canyon to the bare, pointed peaks more than 4,000 feet above it and all the way from Farewell Gap, at the southern end of the valley, to Timber Gap, in the north.

* * *

Walk No. 41 begins in the South Fork Campground, in the southwestern corner of Sequoia National Park. See the description of the Walk on page 187 for directions to the trailhead. Other than the campground, the nearest services to the Walk are in Three Rivers (see above), 13 miles from the trailhead.

* * *

Walk No. 42 is a three-day excursion to Bearpaw Meadow, where you'll spend two nights and enjoy home-cooked meals at the Bearpaw Meadow High Sierra Camp. See the description of the Walk on page 191 for more information.

* * *

All accommodations in the parks (except for campgrounds), as well as those at Stony Creek, in Sequoia National Forest, are operated by the parks' concessioner, Guest Services, Inc. For information and reservations write the company at PO Box 789, Three Rivers, CA 93271 or call 209-561-3314.

Great Walks of Sequoia & Kings Canyon National Parks

1 General Grant Tree Trail

This easy .8-mile Walk takes you through one of the densest concentrations of giant sequoia trees in the parks. You'll see the world's third largest living thing, the 40-foot-thick General Grant Tree, as well as dozens of other sequoias that are as wide as rooms and as tall as office buildings.

The Walk is in Grant Grove. To get to the trailhead from the Grant Grove Visitor Center, take a right onto the Generals Highway. In about .2 miles you'll come to a four-way intersection. Take a left here and follow the winding road that descends into Grant Grove. About .8 miles from the intersection

Giant sequoias loom more than 200 feet above a walker on the **General Grant Tree Trail** *in Grant Grove (Walk No. 1). The white flowers are Western azaleas.*

▶

you'll reach the trailhead parking lot (where there are restrooms with flush toilets). As you drive into the lot, two fused mature sequoias, known as the Twin Sisters, will be on your left and a rare clump of six giant sequoias, called the Happy Family, will be on your right. The paved, counterclockwise loop trail begins straight ahead of you.

At the trailhead, be sure to pick up the *General Grant Grove Trail* pamphlet and map, published by the Sequoia Natural History Association. The 28-page trail guide locates all the named trees in the grove (most of which are named after states of the Union) and describes several of them. It also explains how sequoias grow and how natural fires, far from harming the trees, are actually necessary for their survival.

The Walk, however, is not just informative. It's also lovely. For the sequoias are not only big, they're beautiful: they have warm, cinnamon-colored bark and huge branches covered with green needles. What's more, they share the grove with other evergreen trees, white-flowering dogwoods and large clumps of ceanothus bushes with lavender flowers.

The wide, gentle trail first brings you to the Robert E. Lee Tree. Named after the Confederate general, this 22-foot-wide, 254-foot-high tree is, according to the National Park Service, the world's 12th largest living thing.

Then the trail immediately brings you to the Fallen Monarch, a prostrate tree that extends 125 feet from one arm of the loop trail to the other. The tree's hollow interior is an enormous room—more than 100 feet long, more than six feet high and in some places more than 20 feet wide. At various times in the past century, people lived in it, the US Cavalry stabled horses in it and it even served as a hotel and saloon.

In less than a quarter-mile the trail reaches the General Grant Tree, which, according to the trail guide, is "as tall as a 27-story building, . . . wider at the base than a three-lane highway" and 3.5 feet wider at the base than the world's largest living organism, the General Sherman Tree, in the Giant Forest. If the wood in the nearly 2,000-year-old tree "were strong enough for construction," the pamphlet says, "more than 40 average sized 5-room houses" could be built from it.

At this point turn off the loop trail and start walking clockwise on the paved path that curves around the Grant Tree. In a few hundred feet you'll come to a faint dirt path that leaves the paved trail on the left. (Check the map in the trail guide if you need more reference points.) Follow the unpaved path up the wide gully and then to the right as it climbs up to, then passes through, the Vermont Log, the remains of a 16-foot-thick, 246-foot-high sequoia that fell in 1985.

Now follow the unpaved trail as it curves to the left, around the head of the gully, and enjoy the views of sequoias all around you.

In about .2 miles you'll come to a trail junction near a wooden fence. Keep to the right and in less than .1 miles you'll reach the North Grant View. From here you'll have a rare view of the General Grant Tree from top to bottom.

Now go back to the trail junction, take a right and follow the trail beside the wooden fence. In just a

couple of hundred feet you'll reach the Gamlin Pioneer Cabin, which is beside the paved loop trail. The 16-by-24-foot log cabin was built by the Gamlin brothers in 1872 and later used as a ranger residence. Go inside for a minute and imagine what it was like to live here.

When you come out of the cabin, take a right on the loop trail and you'll quickly come to the Centennial Stump and Log, which is all that remains of an ill-fated moneymaking scheme. According to the trail guide, the Vivian brothers had the tree cut down and a section of it displayed at the American Centennial Exhibition in Philadelphia in 1876. The tree had to be split up before it could be moved, then put back together at the exhibition. Unfortunately, when people saw that the cross-section was not one piece but several, they thought it was a hoax—parts of many trees cobbled together to look like one big one.

The trail passes still more named trees, several of which are described in the trail guide, and, about .2 miles from the cabin, returns to the parking lot.

2 Panoramic Point

This brief .2 mile round trip takes you

Panoramic Point *(Walk No. 2) just before dawn. From this viewpoint in Grant Grove you can see across both Sequoia and Kings Canyon national parks to the Sierra Crest. Hume Lake is in the bottom center.*

◄

quickly to well-named Panoramic Point, site of one of the longest and widest views of the Sierra Nevada on any Great Walk. On few walks can you see so many mountains for so little effort. And if you go another 1.2 miles you'll have even more views to the west and the east.

This Walk is in Grant Grove. To reach the trail-head, turn off the Generals Highway into Grant Grove Village and follow the road past the visitor center and the cabins. Go right at the intersection by Bradley Meadow and follow the narrow paved road as it switches back and forth up the ridge to the east of Grant Grove. You'll drive past large firs and other evergreens and small, lush meadows. About 1.6 miles from the village, the road ends at an unpaved parking area surrounded by large evergreens covered with thick clumps of green staghorn lichen. There are chemical toilets in the woods on the left. On your right is a sign saying that Panoramic Point is 300 yards away.

The four-foot-wide asphalt path winds up the ridge, then makes a long, gentle switchback to Panoramic Point. The point is 7,520 feet high — more than 1,000 feet above Grant Grove. From here you have a 180-degree view: as much as 30 miles to the north, east and south and all the way across both Kings Canyon and Sequoia national parks. Immediately ahead of you is Sequoia National Forest. In the valley below you, and to the left, is Hume Lake. Behind Hume Lake is the canyon of the Middle Fork of the Kings River. Beyond the national forest is Kings Canyon National Park, to your left, and Sequoia National Park, to your right. On the horizon, on the eastern boundary of both parks, are the 2½-mile-high peaks of the Sierra Crest, often snow covered even in summer. Twenty-five summits are identified by a plaque that says, with a simple grandeur fit for the topic: "Before you stretches the Sierra Nevada . . . the Snowy Range." The tallest mountain visible is 14,242-foot North Palisade Peak, in Kings Canyon National Park. Mount Whitney, at 14,495 feet the highest mountain in the continental United States, is hidden behind 13,631-foot Milestone Mountain. Both peaks are in Sequoia National Park.

This view is stunning just before sunrise. It looks like a watercolor, a study in subtle shades of blue and black. The pointed fir trees create a black silhouette against the light blue predawn sky. In the distance, each sharp-edged ridge has its own pure solid color. The mountain horizon is medium blue and each succeeding layer of ridge is a slightly darker hue than the one behind it.

If you'd like to see this view from a slightly different perspective, follow the trail on your right, through chinquapin and manzanita bushes. (Several spur trails leave the main trail on the left. Keep right at intersections as you head south on the Park Ridge Trail.) In about .3 miles you'll reach the crest of the ridge, where you'll have views to both your left and right. Then you'll have occasional views to the east (on your left) as you gradually climb up to a 7,761-foot-high knoll on the ridge. The trail switches back to the right, then to the left and quickly reaches the top of the knoll, about .6 miles from Panoramic

Point. Here, by an outcrop of red quartz on the left of the trail, you'll have another wide view to the east of the ridge. It's not as stunning as the one from Panoramic Point but it's still worth a long look.

After you've enjoyed the vista, turn around and follow the trail back to your car.

3 Windy Cliffs

This undemanding but dramatic three-mile round trip is a little-known delight. It takes you gently up the side of the Windy Cliffs, where you have 180-degree views of the half-mile-high walls of one of the steepest and narrowest sections of Kings Canyon and bird's-eye views of both the South Fork of the Kings River and cascading Boulder Creek. En route you can take a guided tour of Boyden Cavern, where you'll see delicate stalactites and other fascinating formations.

Much of this trail is a narrow shelf carved into very steep slopes. That's one reason this Walk is so dramatic. But the trail may make you uneasy if you're afraid of heights. Also, the path is narrow and often crowded by poison oak

The South Fork of the Kings River surges through Kings Canyon west of **Cedar Grove** *(Walks No. 4–13).*
◄

and other brush, so it's a good idea to wear long pants and long sleeves and to try not to brush against vegetation. If you take this Walk with children, supervise them appropriately.

The Walk is actually in Sequoia National Forest, just west of Cedar Grove in Kings Canyon National Park. To get to the trailhead, take the Kings Canyon Highway west from Cedar Grove Village. In about 10 miles the road crosses from the north to the south side of the Kings River. On the south side of the bridge, on the left, is the Boyden Cavern parking area. At the edge of the parking lot, in the shadow of the Windy Cliffs, is a gift shop, a snack bar and restrooms with chemical toilets.

Both the Walk and the trail to the cave begin at the gift shop/snack bar. If you want to take the 45-minute tour of the cave (see pages 44 and 46), buy your tickets at the snack bar. If you don't want to tour the cave, start walking up the wide, paved path. The walkway follows the Kings River upstream as it gently climbs the steep face of the Windy Cliffs (which are usually not noticeably more windy than any other part of the canyon). You'll have constant views, first to your left, then to your rear, of the nearly vertical walls of the narrow canyon, which rise hundreds of feet up from the river.

About .1 miles from the parking lot the path splits. The paved trail switches back to the right, toward the entrance to the cave. The Windy Cliffs Trail continues straight ahead. A sign here says: "Caution/ Hazardous Trail/Not Maintained." In fact, the trail is washed out in places. But if you take your time and watch your step you should have little difficulty.

Cross over the chain across the trail and follow the now unpaved path as it keeps climbing up the edge of the cliff and temporarily away from the river. You'll have views of the canyon through oaks and bay laurels to your left. Then you'll have views to both your left and right of gray, pointed peaks rising above the canyon.

Soon the trail descends into, then crosses, a usually dry gully known as Windy Gulch. Note the blue-gray marble in the bottom of the ravine.

Then the trail climbs out of the gulch and, as it curves around the face of the cliff, you'll have a dramatic, bird's-eye view of the Kings River and the Kings Canyon Highway, now almost directly below you. Through the clear, shallow water you'll see almost every rock in the bottom of the river. You'll also have 180-degree views up and down the canyon. To your rear you'll see the pointed, gray crags atop the north wall of the canyon, more than 2,000 feet above the river and road below.

The trail is now a narrow, nearly level corniche etched into the Windy Cliffs. The large oaks have all but disappeared and you're surrounded mostly by scrub oaks, tawny grasses and bare rock.

About a mile from the trailhead the path turns right into Boulder Canyon. Now you can see not only up Kings Canyon, to your left, but also up Boulder Canyon and the steep, pointed crags above it. Soon you'll also see Boulder Creek cascading over ledges in the bottom of the canyon, to your left.

Now the trail is a smooth and nearly level shelf in

the steep, grassy slope of the canyon. Soon you'll cross the marble rock of a wash, then you'll enter shady woods. Through the bay laurels and oaks, however, you'll glimpse pools and cascades in Boulder Creek.

Gradually the path moves closer to the creek and, about 1.4 miles from the trailhead, ends at stone-and-cement abutments that once supported a bridge over the creek.

About 200 feet downstream from the former bridge, a 50-foot side trail takes you to a 40-foot-long, 20-foot-wide pool in a ledge in the creek. A cascade flowing into the pool makes it a natural jacuzzi. Unfortunately the water is cold, even in late summer, and the rocks are slippery. If you take a dip, be careful.

When you're ready to return to your car, turn around and follow the path back to the parking lot — and enjoy the views again from another direction.

To get to the cave, take a left when you get back to the paved trail. The tour of the cave begins with a short talk at its entrance. Here you learn that the cavern was first explored in 1906 by Put Boyden, a cook at a logging camp at Hume Lake. Boyden staked a claim to the cave, built a cabin at its entrance and gave tours of the cavern until the winter

The walls of Kings Canyon, the deepest gorge in North America, rise thousands of feet above the South Fork of the Kings River and the Kings Canyon Highway. This view is from the **Windy Cliffs** *(Walk No. 3).*

▶

of 1916, when he froze to death in a blizzard. The cave later became part of the national forest and in 1951 the Forest Service began leasing the site to private concessioners.

The quarter-mile path through the cave is lit with electric lights and guides point out the often intricate formations along the way. Like the more elaborate Crystal Cave (Walk No. 31), near the Giant Forest, Boyden Cavern is open only in late spring, summer and early fall. For more information call 209-736-2708.

4 Hotel Creek Trail

This moderate five-mile round trip takes you up the steep north slope of Kings Canyon, where you'll have continuous views of the glacier-carved valley. You'll also see cascades on Hotel Creek, the two-mile-high peaks of the Monarch Divide and other summits rising above the canyon's south wall.

Much of the Walk is on open, sunny slopes, which provide not only uninterrupted views but also hot and sweaty walking on warm days. If possible, take this Walk on a cool day. If you can't do that, start early in the morning, when the weather is cooler than it is at midday.

The Walk is just north of Cedar Grove Village. To reach the trailhead, simply follow the paved road that goes north from the lodge, toward the clifflike walls of the canyon. In about .2 miles you'll come to an intersection. Take the road to the right, which goes to the stables. You'll barely make your turn before you'll see the trailhead parking area on your left.

Actually, two trails begin here—the Lewis Creek Trail, which goes to the left, and the Hotel Creek Trail, which heads to the right.

The smooth, sandy Hotel Creek Trail climbs easily across a pleasant, almost parklike woods of oaks, pines and a thick carpet of mountain misery, whose small, delicate, complex leaves resemble miniature ferns. You'll soon hear Hotel Creek, on your right, and, just where the trail switches back to the left, you'll see a side path that quickly descends to the creek. Walk down the 40-foot trail to the small stream, go upstream about 30 feet and you'll see a thin, 12-foot-long cascade and a small one below it splashing over ledges in the creek bed.

Now go back to the main trail and start climbing the 33 switchbacks that gently take you 1,200 feet up the steep side of the canyon. So quickly do you climb that you start seeing the south side of the canyon, through oak trees, after only the third switchback.

By the ninth switchback, the oaks have been replaced by large manzanita bushes with reddish-purple woody stems and you begin to have clear, uninterrupted views of the canyon's south walls. The vista includes, from left to right, 10,077-foot Avalanche Peak, 11,254-foot Palmer Mountain, the Roaring River canyon (Walk No. 7), the top of 9,115-foot Sentinel Dome, on the eastern end of the 1.5-mile-long Sentinel Ridge, and 8,531-foot Lookout Peak, on the western end of the ridge.

On some of the switchbacks closest to Hotel Creek you can hear the stream but not quite see it. You can, however, see the ledges of the creek bed.

By the 27th switchback you're high enough to see how this part of Kings Canyon is a little Yosemite — a glacier-carved U-shaped valley consisting of steep, often vertical walls and a flat, evergreen-covered floor. Now you can also glimpse the Kings River meandering through the bottom of the canyon.

By the 31st switchback the slope is less steep, the switchbacks get longer and, because this part of the canyon wall can hold more water than the lower slope, pine trees begin to reappear.

After the last switchback the trail makes a long traverse to the west, descends slightly to a dry creek at the head of a small ravine, crosses the creek and climbs out of the ravine. Your views of the canyon are now mainly through the pines.

Two miles from the trailhead, however, you reach a trail junction, where there are views all around you. The canyon is on your left and the pointed, often snowcapped peaks of the Monarch Divide are on your right, six miles away.

The trail on your right goes to Lewis Creek, the one on your left takes you to an overlook above

---

*The view from the **Hotel Creek Trail** (Walk No. 4) in Cedar Grove: on the horizon, 10,077-foot Avalanche Peak (left) and 11,254-foot Palmer Mountain, both rising above Roaring River canyon (Walk No. 7). Right of the canyon is Sentinel Ridge.*

▶

Cedar Grove. Follow the lefthand trail, which gradually descends along the top of a ridge, past carpets of mountain misery and ceanothus bushes. You'll have more views of Kings Canyon on your left and the Monarch Divide on your right.

Then the trail starts climbing gently up the ridge to a rocky knob beside two Jeffrey pines. This is the Cedar Grove Overlook. You're now more than 1,400 feet above Cedar Grove and you have a nearly 180-degree view up and down Kings Canyon. The vista, from left to right, includes Avalanche Peak, Palmer Mountain, the Roaring River canyon, Sentinel Dome, Sentinel Ridge and Lookout Peak. In the opposite direction is the Monarch Divide.

This overlook has the best view of the entire Walk. It's a perfect place for a picnic, or at least a long pause, before you follow the trail back to your car.

5 Don Cecil Trail

This undemanding two-mile round trip takes you gently up the south slope of Kings Canyon, through almost parklike woods, to a vista of the Monarch Divide and other bare, pointed two-mile-high peaks. You'll also cross Sheep Creek where it slides into a picturesque 100-foot-deep gorge.

The Walk begins at the trailhead sign on the south side of the Kings Canyon Highway, less than .2 miles east of the road to Cedar Grove Village.

Park beside the Kings Canyon Highway, then follow the very smooth trail to the left, up the even, evergreen-shaded slope. The path switches back to the right after a couple of hundred feet and begins a long climbing traverse of the valley wall. You'll walk past incense-cedars, pines, oaks and mountain misery.

About a quarter-mile from the trailhead you'll cross an unpaved park service road, then an often dry creek, as the smooth, needle-coated path winds through a clean, almost parklike forest of young trees.

In about three-quarters of a mile you'll reach an overlook that's more than 500 feet above the bottom of the canyon. From here you have a 90-degree view of Sierra peaks north of Cedar Grove. The vista, from left to right, includes the 9,649-foot Eagle Peaks, the Grand Dike in front of them, 11,009-foot Mount Harrington, 11,077-foot Hogback Peak, 10,915-foot Slide Peak and 11,473-foot Mount Kennedy — all landmarks of the Monarch Divide — Kennedy Pass and the bare summits of the 11,618-foot Comb Spur and 10,785-foot Mount Hutchings. Below the mountains is the long canyon of Lewis Creek, which flows into the South Fork of Kings River. On the western end of the ridge just across the canyon is the Cedar Grove Overlook (Walk No. 4).

The trail now descends quickly into the narrow, picturesque 100-foot-deep rock gorge of Sheep Creek. From the sturdy wooden bridge over the gorge you can see cascades both up- and downstream.

After you've enjoyed this intriguing view of dark

ledge and white water, turn around and follow the path back to your car. On your way take another long look at the view of the mountains on the other side of Kings Canyon.

6 Knapp's Cabin

This quick and very easy 300-foot Walk — the second shortest Great Walk in the parks after No. 9 — takes you to the oldest building in Cedar Grove and to a pleasant vista of the Kings River and the steep walls of the canyon beyond it.

The Walk begins in a parking area on the north side of the Kings Canyon Highway, about two miles east of the road to Cedar Grove Village. The trail begins just a few feet from the sign saying "Knapp's Cabin."

Follow the 150-foot-long path through the trees to the top of a low rise. Here you'll find a handsome, well-built and well-maintained one-room cabin. It's framed not with two-by-fours but with the trunks of small trees, and both its roof and walls are faced with weathered wood shingles. A plaque explains that

The near-vertical walls of the glacier-carved Kings Canyon in **Cedar Grove** *(Walks No. 4–13), seen just before dawn at Canyon View on the Kings Canyon Highway.*

▶

George O. Knapp wasn't just another dirt-poor homesteader or trapper but a "wealthy California businessman" who "conducted several elaborate summer camping trips" in the area. The plaque says the cabin was built "during the 'Roaring Twenties'" as a "storage shed" for Knapp's "expeditions."

About 50 feet from the cabin you can see the Kings River rushing over a wide, rocky bed. Above the river rise the high, nearly vertical rock walls of the canyon.

After you've enjoyed the view, follow the path back to your car.

7 Roaring River Falls

This easy .4-mile round trip takes you to one of the most exciting water features in the parks: a waterfall surging into a deep green pool ringed by cliffs.

The Walk begins in a parking area on the south side of the Kings Canyon Highway, just east of the bridge over Roaring River and about 2.5 miles east of the road to Cedar Grove Village.

Take the nearly level, four-foot-wide asphalt trail, which follows Roaring River upstream. In about .2 miles the path ends at the pool at the base of the falls.

You're now in a vast rock bowl. Steep rock cliffs rise hundreds of feet on both sides of the river and form the curving, nearly vertical walls of the 60-foot-wide pool. The cliffs and the deep green pool are the setting for the jewel of the composition: a cascade that surges, in a long curve, through a narrow notch in the ledge above the pool and makes a 25-foot leap into the nearly circular basin. The fall is a thick, churning triangular column of white water, about six feet wide where it pours out of the notch and about 20 feet wide where it crashes into the pool. It hits the pool so hard that it creates a three-foot-high mound of white foam at the base of the cataract. It also makes waves that ripple over the entire surface of the pool and it produces a thick mist that can be felt by bystanders more than 100 feet away. Though the effects of the falls are a picture of complexity, the entire composition is simplicity itself, made up essentially of just three elements: the curving gray rock bowl, the round green pool and, in the center of everything, the white falls.

The falls, incidentally, are just the climax of a series of cascades that extend for more than 200 feet upstream in the river's steep, narrow rock canyon. Only the final falls, however, are visible.

If you'd like to see the falls from another perspective, follow the path back to the road and cross the bridge over the river. On the other side of the bridge, on the south side of the road, you'll see an unpaved path. Follow it upstream, through an open woods of small oaks and many rocks. In about 200 feet the path curves to the left and passes a high ledge, on your right. Then it follows stone steps to an overlook. From here you can see the falls, the green pool below them and many smaller pools and cascades downstream.

Enjoy the view, then retrace your route back to your car.

8 Zumwalt Meadow

The 1.5-mile Zumwalt Meadow Nature Trail is an easy, mostly level and informative Walk around a lush quarter-mile-long meadow. En route you'll learn how the meadow was created and why it will someday die. You'll also be introduced to the plants, trees and animals that live in and around it and you'll have views of the Kings River, Lion Head, North Dome and the Grand Sentinel.

The Walk begins in a parking area on the south side of the Kings Canyon Highway, about .9 miles from the end of the highway and about 4.5 miles east of the road to Cedar Grove Village. Buy a copy of the pamphlet, *Zumwalt Nature Trail,* in the box on the wooden sign at the trailhead. It describes what you'll see at numbered stops along the trail. (If the box is empty, you can get a pamphlet at the ranger station in Cedar Grove Village.)

The path, carpeted at first by ponderosa pine needles, begins by following the Kings River downstream. Here the river, on your left, is shallow and

The South Fork of the Kings River and the granite cliffs of Kings Canyon seen from **Knapp's Cabin** *(Walk No. 6) in Cedar Grove.*

▶

unusually smooth. Through the clear water you can see how the riverbed is lined with small stones. Across the river is Zumwalt Meadow and looming more than 4,000 feet above it is the 8,504-foot Grand Sentinel. On the south side of the valley, on your right, is 8,717-foot North Dome and the smaller peak to the right of it known as Lion Head.

In just a couple of hundred feet you'll come to trail marker no. 4. In the low granite ledges about 40 feet to the right of the trail you'll see six bedrock mortars. As the pamphlet explains, these round holes, three to seven inches wide at the top, were used by Indian women to grind acorns into flour for mush or bread, both staples of the Indian diet. Walk about 40 feet past the mortars and you'll come to a plaque commemorating Jesse and Abraham Agnew, two California pioneers.

Less than .2 miles from the trailhead you'll reach a suspension bridge over the Kings River. From the bridge you can look down at the gold-colored rocks beneath the gray-green water.. You also have a clear view of the meadow upstream and the steep canyon walls beyond it.

Go left at the trail junction on the other side of the bridge. You now have another view of North Dome, whose south face (as the trail guide explains) was polished smooth by the 1,600-foot-deep glacier that once filled this valley. You'll also see a lovely composition on your left: the softly flowing river surrounded by the green meadow—a focal point within a focal point—the meadow ringed by trees and the entire floor of the valley surrounded by the evergreen-festooned canyon walls.

The trail next crosses tiny, often dry Sentinel Creek, passes through a shady white fir forest and winds through rough talus, or rocks, broken off the steep lower slope of the Grand Sentinel, on your right. Here you have continuous views of the meadow and North Dome and Lion Head beyond it.

Then the trail passes a small marsh, goes by another talus slope, on the right of the trail, and comes to another trail junction. Follow the path to the left, between two cabin-size boulders and across a small grassy area, then into a pine and incense-cedar woods and along the Kings River. Through the evergreens on your left you'll see the meadow.

Soon the trail leaves the evergreens behind and emerges onto the sunny meadow. Here you'll have still more views of the Grand Sentinel, on your left.

Then the path crosses the wet western end of the meadow on a 150-foot boardwalk. Take your time here to enjoy the meadow—now on both sides of you—and the continuous views in all directions.

Immediately after the boardwalk the path crosses Sentinel Creek on a wooden bridge near trail stop no. 6. You've now completed a nearly one-mile loop. From here you simply retrace your steps to your car.

9 Grand Sentinel View

This quick and easy 200-foot round trip—easily the shortest Great Walk in the parks—takes you to the banks of the Kings River,

where you'll have an especially close view of a Cedar Grove landmark.

The Walk begins in a parking area on the south side of the Kings Canyon Highway, about .6 miles from the end of the road and about five miles east of the road to Cedar Grove Village.

The needle-carpeted path begins near the middle of the parking area and runs under pines and incense-cedars to the north bank of the river, which is 50 feet wide here and briskly flowing. Look up and you'll see, less than a quarter of a mile away, the nearly vertical cliffs of the Grand Sentinel. At the top of the cliffs you'll also see the three summits of the 8,504-foot promontory.

There are usually few, if any, people here. So if you're looking for a pretty place for a quiet lunch, this riparian vantage point usually suffices.

When you're ready to return to your car, simply follow the path back to the parking area.

10 Sentinel Trail

This undemanding five-mile round trip parallels the south bank of the Kings River. It offers vistas of the Grand Sentinel, Sentinel

The 25-foot-high **Roaring River Falls** *(Walk No. 7) plunge into a 60-foot-wide pool in Cedar Grove.*
◄

Dome, Lion Head, Muir's Pulpit and Buck Peak and close views of the Kings River and cascading Bubbs Creek.

This Walk is part of the Walk to Mist Falls (No. 11). If you plan to take that Walk you may want to skip this one.

The Sentinel Trail begins near the end of the Kings Canyon Highway, about 5.5 miles east of the road to Cedar Grove Village. To get to the trailhead, start driving around the one-way loop near the end of the road and immediately turn into the parking area on the right. You'll enter the parking area at its northwestern corner. The trailhead is near the southwestern corner; a sign there says, among other things, that Bubbs Creek is 2.6 miles away.

The smooth, level trail passes briefly through evergreens and reaches a usually unmarked junction in just .1 miles. Go right. You're now in an open area and you'll see peaks all around you: the Grand Sentinel on your left, Sentinel Dome and Lion Head on your right and 8,776-foot Buck Peak behind you. To the right of Buck Peak is 11,154-foot Glacier Monument.

In about a quarter-mile from the trailhead you'll cross the Kings River on a footbridge. Below the bridge is a large green pool. So clear is the river that it's almost invisible; it looks less like water than a dry riverbed of green-tinted sand and stones.

Take a left at the trail junction on the other side of the river and follow the Kings upstream. Now you'll have views of the picturesque aqua pools and gravelly beaches in the softly flowing stream and you'll have more vistas of North Dome, Lion Head, the Grand Sentinel, Buck Peak and the Glacier Monument.

The trail then enters evergreen woods but you'll still have glimpses, through the trees, of the river and the bare rock promontories on both sides of the canyon.

In about .5 miles you'll have a view, to your rear, of the enormous boulder known as Muir's Pulpit (Walk No. 12), on the north bank of the river. If the day is warm you may see swimmers jumping off it. If the day is cool, fishermen may be casting from it instead.

Then the trail goes away from the river and through a wide, flat, sunny clearing. Soon you'll pass an enormous rock, about 40 feet high and 50 feet long, just to the right of the trail. Painted on the rock, about six feet off the ground, are the intials "W. B." From the middle of the B a thick arrow points to the right, or west, and below the initials is the date "1912." No one knows who W. B. was but apparently he was trying to say that he passed here, heading west, in 1912.

Immediately after the boulder the trail crosses a rocky moraine, which stretches across the path like a small dam. Then the trail passes through a sandy area covered with thousands of stones. Like the moraine, the rocks were dropped here by a glacier. In this open area, where only pines and manzanita bushes grow, you can see the Grand Sentinel, North Dome, Lion Head and Buck Peak.

Now the trail goes into the woods and follows the creek for about a quarter-mile. Then it enters a small, sunny meadow, where you have more views of Buck Peak and the Grand Sentinel.

The trail next passes through a wet woods, thick with ferns. Here you'll see a small marsh, dense with willows, on your left.

The path then winds through sunnier, drier woods and crosses a creek flowing slowly over a wide, rocky bed.

Next you cross several often dry creeks and, about 2.5 miles from the trailhead, reach a trail junction just before another unnamed creek. You're now near the junction of Bubbs Creek and the Kings River and the sounds of water are continuous.

In a few minutes you'll take the trail on the left, which goes to the Kings River. Right now, however, go straight ahead, cross the creek and walk about 60 feet to the footbridge over Bubbs Creek. The creek is a major tributary of the Kings River and the bridge provides a good view of its powerful cascades. Look upstream and you'll see the creek flowing around an island like a necklace.

Go back to the trail junction, take a right and follow the path along the unnamed creek to the Kings River. In about .1 miles you'll come to the gray steel Bailey bridge over the river. From the 100-

---

The peaks of the 9,146-foot Sphinx seen on the trail to **Mist Falls** *(Walk No. 11) in Cedar Grove. The peaks are named for the rock formation at the top of the highest summit. The formation has a man's head and a lion's body, just like an Egyptian sphinx.*

▶

foot-long span you can see, in almost every direction, the steep cliffs of Kings Canyon. Buck Peak is to the north, the slopes of the 9,146-foot Sphinx are to the south, the Grand Sentinel is to the southwest and the Glacier Monument is to the east. You can also see several hundred feet up and down the river, here about 60 feet wide but only one or two feet deep. About 150 feet upstream Bubbs Creek makes a long sheet of white foam as it surges into the Kings.

When you're ready, turn around at the bridge and retrace your steps to your car.

11 Mist Falls

This moderately strenuous nine-mile round trip is the second longest Great Walk in the parks (after the trip to Bearpaw Meadow High Sierra Camp) but it's also one of the most rewarding. It takes you along the cascading Kings River to 50-foot-high Mist Falls. On the way you'll have views of the Grand Sentinel, Sentinel Dome, Lion Head, Muir's Pulpit, Buck Peak, the Glacier Monument and Bubbs Creek and you'll enjoy grand vistas down the Kings River canyon to the summits of the Sphinx.

For its first 2.5 miles, this Walk follows the route of the Sentinel Trail (Walk No. 10). When you reach the turnaround point of Walk No. 10 — the Bailey bridge over the Kings River—continue across the bridge and follow the trail to the left. In about 100 feet you'll come to a trail junction. The left trail goes back to the end of the Kings Canyon Highway. The right trail starts climbing up through the rough talus along the northwest side of the Kings River.

Go right. You'll soon see the Bailey bridge over the river, far to your right, and, upstream from the bridge, the foaming mouth of Bubbs Creek. Rising on both sides of the path are the steep walls of the Kings River canyon. The 8,776-foot Buck Peak is on your left and the 11,154-foot Glacier Monument is on your right.

The trail then goes away from the river and passes a moist area, on the right, thick with horsetails, ferns and willows.

Next the trail climbs through more talus, then through a mixed woods (of both evergreen and deciduous trees) before coming back beside the river. Now you have almost constant views, through trees, of both the river and the peaks of the Sphinx behind you.

About a mile from the trail junction you climb over more talus and you can see the river rush over wide ledges in long white flumes and three-, four- and five-foot-high waterfalls.

Then the well-made trail winds briefly above and away from the river on ledge, from which you have an open view of the Sphinx. The trail then goes back to the creek, where you see more falls and cascades.

Next it switchbacks higher up the wide, open ledge, where you have a classic Sierra view. Down-

stream the steep walls of the canyon create a deep V shape. In the middle of the V rise the massive peaks of the 9,146-foot Sphinx, named after the rock formation on the left (eastern) slope of its rightmost peak. The rock figure, which looks like an Egyptian sphinx, has the body of a reclining lion and the head of a man, looking east. Below the Sphinx and spread across the bottom of the canyon are rolling evergreen forests bisected by the cascading river. This is the best view on the Walk. Pause for a while and take a long look.

Now the trail passes a massive, four-foot-thick Jeffrey pine. Its luxuriant branches reach the ground and form an arch under which you walk.

As the trail keeps climbing gently up beside the Kings River, you come to many ledges providing bird's-eye views of the river as it slides smoothly over wide rocks, drops in numberless falls and cascades and makes a white froth as it churns through round potholes.

Finally, two miles from the Bailey bridge, you reach a trail junction marked with a metal sign announcing the presence of Mist Falls. The left trail goes to Paradise Valley, the right trail to the falls. Take a right and, as you start walking down toward the river, you'll have your first view of the cascades.

The falls are created by a large ledge, about 35 feet wide and 50 feet high, that bestrides the canyon like a

---

Mist Falls *(Walk No. 11) pour over a ledge in the Kings River in Cedar Grove.*
◄

dam. The river slides gently down the top part of the ledge "dam," then drops more precipitously down the steeper bottom part in dozens of small, one- to three-foot-high falls and several 25-foot-high cataracts. There are so many falls that the larger ones leap over smaller ones, creating layers of water. Below the falls the river creates another 150 feet of small cascades and rapids as it spills over countless large and small rocks.

You can watch this rock-and-water show from a flat, 25-foot-long triangle-shaped rock at the edge of the river, about 100 feet below the falls. From this comfortable perch you can also feel how the falls got their name: The numberless cataracts make so much mist that the spray sometimes rises above the falls themselves and travels as far as the rock. From here you can also see the long, thin ribbon of Gardiner Creek cascading down the steep rock wall of the other side of the canyon into the Kings River.

If you'd like an even closer view of the falls you can walk a few feet farther upstream and climb — carefully — up on a boulder near the shallow green pool that stretches across the base of the cascades.

Mist Falls is an excellent spot for a picnic. Tarry a while before you turn around and follow the path back to your car. On your return trip you'll have even more views of the Sphinx because you'll be walking "into" them.

When you reach the trail junction by the Bailey bridge over the Kings River you may be tempted to take the right path back to your car because it's about .5 miles shorter than the Sentinel Trail. Resist the temptation. The trail has no views of the Kings

River or, for that matter, of any other interesting features that you can't see elsewhere, and it goes over mostly open, sandy flats that make for sweaty, tedious trudging, especially at the end of a warm day.

12 Muir's Pulpit

This very easy .1-mile round trip takes you to the gigantic boulder in the Kings River on which the famed conservationist John Muir addressed members of the Sierra Club. The rock, now known as Muir Rock or Muir's Pulpit, also has a grand view of the Grand Sentinel.

The Walk begins on the south side of the parking area on the southern arc of the loop at the end of the Kings Canyon Highway. The trailhead is about 5.5 miles from the road to Cedar Grove Village and just a few feet east of the Mist Falls trailhead.

A plaque near the Muir's Pulpit trailhead explains that John Muir worked to preserve what he called this "surpassingly glorious region for the recreation and well-being of humanity." As part of his efforts, Muir often spoke to his fellow Sierra Club members on what is now called Muir Rock or Muir's Pulpit.

The nearly level trail to the boulder runs beneath incense-cedars and pines and, less than 250 feet from the parking area, reaches the Pulpit. Resting on the north bank of the Kings River, the rock is immense—about 40 feet across and 50 feet long—and its top is nearly flat and gently sloping, like a tiny

auditorium—perfect for Muir and his audience to get a good view of each other.

The rock is also a fine place to look at the aqua-colored river, which here is smooth, deep and 60 feet wide, and it offers a close view of the Grand Sentinel, looming almost 3,500 feet above the river.

When you're ready to return to your car, follow the path back to the parking lot.

13 Copper Creek Trail

This moderate 1.5-mile round trip takes you quickly up the steep north wall of Kings Canyon, where you have open and continuous views of the Grand Sentinel, Buck Peak, North Dome, Lion Head, the Sphinx and the flat, evergreen-covered floor of the canyon.

Like the Hotel Creek Trail (Walk No. 4), this Walk is on open, sunny slopes. On warm days, it can be hot and sweaty. So try to take it on a cool day. If you can't, start early in the morning, when the weather is cooler. (And if you want to walk even farther up the trail, bring along enough extra food and water.)

The Walk begins in a parking area on the north

The peaks of the massive 8,504-foot Grand Sentinel seen from the **Copper Creek Trail** *(Walk No. 13) in Cedar Grove.*
◄

arc of the one-way loop at the end of the Kings Canyon Highway. The parking area is about 5.6 miles east of the road to Cedar Grove Village and just a few hundred feet after the park information cabin.

Like the Hotel Creek Trail, this trail is smooth, sandy, well-built and gently graded. Also like the Hotel Creek Trail, the path heads upward and to the right, then switches back and forth up the steep canyon wall. You first pass through an open woods of pines, oaks and manzanita bushes. But the pines soon disappear, the oaks get fewer and smaller and, as a result, the views become more and more open. So quickly (but gently) does the trail climb the steep canyon wall that your vistas broaden with almost every step you take. You barely begin walking before you can see the steep, bare ledge of the 8,504-foot Grand Sentinel, on the other side of the canyon. After only the first switchback you can see the slope of 8,717-foot North Dome, to the west, and 8,776-foot Buck Peak, to the east, on the other side of Copper Creek canyon.

After only the third switchback you can see the white water of Bubbs Creek, to the southeast. After just the fifth switchback you can see the rock promontory known as Lion Head, below North Dome. Here too you get your first look at the flat, evergreen-carpeted floor of Kings Canyon, the steep, rock wall of Copper Creek canyon and, to the right of Bubbs Creek, the three summits of the Sphinx.

After the sixth switchback you can see farther up and down the canyon floor. Here you keenly sense the scale of the mile-wide Grand Sentinel. Directly opposite you and less than a half-mile away, it's the broadest, most massive thing you can see from the trail.

After the eighth switchback you see more of the smooth vertical cliffs of Copper Creek canyon and the evergreen-festooned ledges of the lower slopes of Buck Peak. You'll also hear and may even catch a glimpse of Copper Creek, deep in the canyon to the east.

After the ninth switchback you'll quickly come to a flat ledge with a boulder resting on it. You've now walked about three-quarters of a mile and you've seen the best views of Kings Canyon that this trail has to offer. This is therefore a good spot to stop, rest and enjoy the view (and perhaps a snack) before turning around and savoring the wide-open vistas all over again on your way back to your car. The changing position of the sun will constantly change the light on, and therefore the colors of, the rock peaks. See if you notice these subtle changes on your way down the trail.

If you feel like a longer walk, you can keep following the switchbacks up the canyon wall. Your views of Kings Canyon, however, will gradually be replaced by the less dramatic views of Cooper Creek canyon.

14 Redwood Canyon

This easy two-mile Walk takes you to dense concentrations of giant sequoias in the largest sequoia grove in the world. You'll also see the remains of an old sequoia logging camp and a cabin made from a giant sequoia trunk.

The Walk is in Kings Canyon National Park, about 6.7 miles from the Grant Grove Visitor Center. To get to the trailhead, take the Generals Highway to the four-way intersection in Quail Flat, which is about 5.3 miles southeast of the visitor center and about four miles southeast of the three-way intersection of the Generals Highway and Route 180 south of Grant Grove. At the four-way intersection the road to Hume Lake goes north and the road to the Redwood Saddle goes south.

Follow the narrow, unpaved road to the Redwood Saddle, which winds along a shelf cut into the steep slope of Redwood Canyon. In about a mile you'll enter the Redwood Mountain Grove and you'll pass many giant sequoias. A lot of them are growing so close to the road that you can almost touch them as you go by. In fact, the views of sequoias from your car rival the views you'll see on the Walk.

About 1.7 miles from the Generals Highway the road comes to the Redwood Saddle and forks in front of a fallen sequoia. Take the left fork and, in about .1 miles, you'll come to a parking area encircled by giant sequoias. Here you'll see a wooden signboard with maps and descriptions of both Redwood Mountain and Redwood Canyon trails.

A walker enjoys the panoramic view from 8,211-foot **Big Baldy** *(Walk No. 16).*

▶

To the left of the signboard is an old road that takes you to trails leading to the Hart Tree and Redwood Canyon. Follow the road as it gradually descends into the canyon, past sequoias on both sides of you. Through the trees you'll see Buena Vista Peak (Walk No. 15) straight ahead and Big Baldy (Walk No. 16) to the right.

In less than .5 miles you'll come to a trail junction. Take the Redwood Creek Trail to the right and follow it briefly down Redwood Canyon, parallel to Redwood Creek, past firs, dogwoods, wild strawberries and, of course, lots of giant sequoias. After about .2 miles, however, the big trees become few and far between and without them, unfortunately, the woods are just another forest. So turn around here, return to the trail junction and go right on the Hart Tree Trail, which gently descends through a dense stand of giant sequoias.

About .4 miles from the junction you'll cross Redwood Creek on stones. On the other side of the creek are the remains of a logging camp known as Barton's Post Camp. On your left you'll see two sequoia stumps, both about 12 feet wide and 20 feet high. How were lumbermen able to cut the trees so high off the ground? They stood on wooden scaffolding. You can see several holes, each about four inches deep and four to six inches wide, that were cut to hold the scaffolding. You can also see fallen trees and other logging debris in the camp, including one tree cut only partway through.

Keep following the trail, to the left of the two stumps, and you'll soon pass more stumps and fallen sequoias, including one 10-foot-thick, 100-foot-long tree that lies prostrate along the right side of the path.

You'll soon cross a tiny creek and immediately come to the remains of a structure that's truly a log cabin. It's a fallen 50-foot-long sequoia hollowed out by fire. Inside the tree is a 40-foot-long room, tall enough to stand in and nine feet across at its widest point. Its openings are closed off with wooden shingles and there's a fieldstone fireplace at one end. Sequoia log cabins like this one were often used as houses by loggers, ranchers and other early inhabitants of the Sierra. Another one, Tharp's Log, is in the Giant Forest. You'll see it on Walk No. 29.

After you've inspected this unusual but rain-tight shelter turn around and follow the trail back to your car.

15 Buena Vista Peak

This undemanding two-mile round trip takes you to the top of 7,603-foot Buena Vista Peak. En route you'll have views of Buck Rock and peaks to the north. On the summit you'll see peaks in all directions, including Big Baldy, the Silliman Crest, Redwood Mountain and the foothills to the south.

The Walk is in Kings Canyon National Park. It begins in a parking area on the west side of the Generals Highway, about 6.5 miles from the Grant Grove Visitor Center, about 5.2 miles southeast of

the intersection of the Generals Highway and Route 180, and about 200 feet south of the Kings Canyon Overlook, on the east side of the road. An incised brown-stained wood sign near the road says "Buena Vista Trail."

Walk through the opening in the split-rail fence and follow the smooth trail through an open woods of incense-cedar, pine and fir. The path climbs briefly through thick stands of lupine, then ascends more gradually as it passes through a cluster of a half-dozen room-size boulders resting on ledge like huge outdoor sculptures.

Then the trail passes over more ledges and over sometimes sandy, sometimes grassy open slopes. Here you'll find manzanita and ceanothus bushes instead of evergreen trees. On your left you can see the bare, gray peaks of the Monarch Divide, more than 15 miles away. To the right of the peaks, on the horizon, is the 8,500-foot rock tower known as Buck Rock (Walk No. 17). With binoculars you can see a cabin on top of the rock that's used as a fire lookout.

Soon you'll also see the gray, rounded dome of Buena Vista Peak straight ahead and you'll have even better views of the mountains to your left. You'll be able to pick out 10,051-foot Spanish Mountain, the 9,700-foot Obelisk to its right and even more peaks of the Monarch Divide.

The smooth path then goes into a lush, shady grove of both young and old fir trees on the north

Sunset on the trail to **Big Baldy** *(Walk No. 16).*
◄

side of Buena Vista Peak (which is now on your right).

Then the trail curves around toward the east side of the peak, passes through more open woods of manzanita and ceanothus and climbs up the ridge on the east side of the summit. On your left, to the south-southeast, you'll see the long ridge, ledgy slopes and spurs of 8,209-foot Big Baldy (Walk No. 16).

Then the trail makes an earnest but brief climb to the top of Buena Vista Peak. The summit is a pleasant place, furnished with handsome pines and manzanitas and boulders resting on black-speckled white granite ledge. Although you're only about 300 feet higher than the parking lot you can see in all directions. To the left of Big Baldy is the steep, bare Silliman Crest, which marks the boundary of Kings Canyon and Sequoia national parks. To the left of the crest is the wide, 9,594-foot Shell Mountain. To the left of Shell Mountain is Buck Rock and two-mile-high peaks to the north and northeast. To the west is Redwood Canyon (Walk No. 14), home of thousands of giant sequoias. Beyond the canyon is Redwood Mountain. To the south is 4,927-foot Yucca Mountain, the 5,612-foot Ash Peaks and the layers of ridges in the foothills south of Sequoia National Park. Each ridge is a slightly lighter blue than the ridge in front of it.

Buena Vista means "good view" in Spanish and the peak is well named. Its vistas are worth a long look and they make the peak a fine place for a picnic. After you've enjoyed the summit, follow the trail back to your car.

16 Big Baldy

This moderate 4.6-mile round trip offers panoramic views from 8,209-foot Big Baldy and often continuous vistas en route. You'll see Redwood Canyon, Redwood Mountain, Buena Vista Peak, Buck Rock, Little Baldy, the Silliman Crest, the Great Western Divide and other two-mile-high Sierra peaks. If you walk a half-mile beyond Big Baldy you'll also see Chimney Rock.

The Walk begins on the Generals Highway in the Sequoia National Forest, just outside Kings Canyon National Park. The trailhead is about eight miles southeast of the Grant Grove Visitor Center and 6.7 miles southeast of the intersection of the Generals Highway and Route 180. It's also about 4.5 miles northwest of Stony Creek Village and just a few hundred feet west of the intersection of the Generals Highway and the road to Big Meadows. The parking turnoff is on the south side of the road and it's marked by a wooden sign saying "Big Baldy Trailhead."

The trail follows a long north-south ridge that forms the east wall of Redwood Canyon (Walk No. 14) and runs all the way from the trailhead to Big Baldy.

At first the smooth trail runs through open, sunny woods. Through the trees on your right you'll have views into Redwood Canyon and of Redwood Mountain beyond. To the right of Redwood Mountain are the open, ledgy slopes of Buena Vista Peak (Walk No. 15).

As the trail climbs gradually up the steep west slope of the ridge, the vista expands to a 180-degree panorama. You'll have a continuous view not only of Redwood Canyon, Redwood Mountain and Buena Vista Peak but also of the two-mile-high peaks in Kings Canyon National Park in the north and the rolling foothills in the southern part of Sequoia National Park. After about three-quarters of a mile the trail reaches the crest of the ridge and enters shady woods. Here you briefly have views, to your left, of the Tableland and the Silliman Crest to the east.

In about a mile the trail comes out of the woods at a sunny point covered with manzanita bushes. Here too you have a 180-degree view. Look straight ahead and you can see Big Baldy. It's a rough, bare rock knob farther south on the ridge and surrounded by evergreens. To the right of Big Baldy are ledge spurs—small ridges with pointed spines—that run down from the larger ridge. The five-mile-long, evergreen-forested Redwood Canyon is on your right.

The nearly level trail remains largely in the open for at least another .5 miles and, as it runs over sunny ledges and between manzanita bushes, it provides more uninterrupted views to the south and west and occasional views to the east.

Now the trail climbs briefly through woods on the east side of the ridge, then levels off and emerges onto an open area where you have a 200-degree vista that includes, from right to left, the ridge where you just walked, the stone pinnacle of 8,500-foot Buck Rock (Walk No. 17) — use binoculars for a close view of the fire lookout cabin on the top — the peaks of the Monarch Divide, Buena Vista Peak, Redwood Mountain, the southern foothills and, ahead of you, the buttresslike rock slopes and bare rock dome of Big Baldy.

The trail then switches back and forth as it makes a brief but earnest climb to the top of Big Baldy. Here you are 8,209 feet high and you have 360-degree views. You can see everything you saw earlier on the Walk plus the dome of 8,044-foot-high Little Baldy (Walk No. 19) to the southeast and, to the left of Little Baldy, the often snowcapped peaks of the Great Western Divide, the long, bare ridges of the Tableland and the Silliman Crest to the east and the peaks of the Sierra Crest to the northeast.

You've now walked about 2.3 miles and the views from here are the best on the Walk. If, however, you'd like to see still more vistas from the ridge and don't mind adding another mile to your excursion, follow the now stony trail down from Big Baldy, then through open woods on the crest of the ridge. You'll have views both left and right of the trail.

About .5 miles from Big Baldy you'll climb up a rocky knob, from which you can see the well-named Chimney Rock to the east. Five miles directly beyond the 7,711-foot granite column is Little Baldy. Other summits, high and low, are almost all around you. (Most of the mountains, however, are far away and many of them are seen much better from Little Baldy.)

When you're ready, turn around and follow the

trail back to your car. If you have time, pause at Big Baldy for another long look at the view.

Incidentally, the sunset from the beginning of the Big Baldy Trail is often brilliant. If the sky is clear, if you're in the area late in the day and if you feel like a short twilight walk, go less than a quarter-mile up the trail, to where you have a wide view of Redwood Canyon and Redwood Mountain, and enjoy the setting sun. You'll have plenty of time to walk back to your car before dark but bring along a flashlight in case you want to linger.

17 Buck Rock

This .2-mile round trip—one of the easiest Great Walks in the area—takes you to 8,500-foot Buck Rock, where you have a 90-degree view of the peaks to the north of Kings Canyon. If the fire lookout on top of Buck Rock is open, you'll have a 360-degree view that includes Buena Vista Peak, Redwood Mountain and Big Baldy. You'll also enjoy many vistas on your drive to Buck Rock, including the Great Western Divide, Shell Mountain and Castle Rocks.

Buck Rock is in the Sequoia National Forest, between Sequoia and Kings Canyon national parks and about five miles from the Generals Highway. To get to the trailhead, turn north off the Generals

Highway onto the road to Big Meadows, at an intersection about eight miles southeast of the Grant Grove Visitor Center. The intersection is also about 6.7 miles southeast of the junction of the Generals Highway and Route 180, about 4.4 miles northwest of Stony Creek Village and just a few hundred feet east of the Big Baldy trailhead (Walk No. 16). It's marked by a brown-stained sign with incised yellow letters.

In about 2.8 miles the road to Big Meadows forks. Go left and follow the now-unpaved but smooth road through the Buck Rock Campground.

The road then climbs up an open, sunny ridge and you'll start seeing landmarks to the east: first the long mound of 9,594-foot Shell Mountain, less than five miles away, then the 12,000-foot summits of the Great Western Divide, then 8,044-foot Little Baldy (Walk No. 19). Twenty miles to the northeast are the summits of the Sierra Crest. Nine miles to the south are the 9,081-foot Castle Rocks, on the south wall of the canyon of the Middle Fork of the Kaweah River. Ahead of you, to the left of the road, is Buck Rock.

About five miles from the Generals Highway, near a radio tower on a knoll to your left, the road splits into three narrower dirt roads. Park just before the intersection, making sure you don't block any traffic, then walk up the middle road, which is identified by a Forest Service sign as number 13S04B.

In about 100 feet you'll come to a green metal gate that bars the road to cars. Walk past the gate and follow the nearly level road through evergreens as it winds to the left, around the edge of the ridge. You'll continue having views to the east, through the trees.

As you round the northern edge of the ridge, you'll see, first, the bare summits of the Monarch Divide, then, to the left of the divide, the 9,700-foot Obelisk and, left of the Obelisk, 10,051-foot Spanish Mountain.

Then you'll see Buck Rock ahead of you. The rock is a massive granite column on the west side of the ridge that towers above the ridge itself and stands as much as 2,500 feet above the national forest below it. On top of the rock is a fire lookout cabin.

The path quickly takes you up the base of the rock. Then you climb wooden steps to a cement landing with an iron gate across it. If the tower is occupied the gate will be unlocked and you can ascend the steps that zigzag up the rock to the cabin. If no one is in the cabin you'll have to stop at the landing. But the view from the landing is one of the best in the area. Four miles to your left is Hume Lake and the Kings Canyon Highway, switching back and forth down Kings Canyon. Beyond the canyon, to the north-west, is Rodgers Ridge. To the right of the ridge is Spanish Mountain and the Obelisk and, farther to the right, the bare summits of the Monarch Divide. In the distance are the peaks of the Sierra Crest. If Buck Rock were several thousand feet higher you'd be able to see into the bottom of Kings Canyon, which runs east-west, across the vista. As it is you can only distinguish its northern and southern slopes — the north one is gray green and looks much fainter than the rich dark green forests on the southern slope. To the northeast, on the south slope of the canyon, is 8,531-foot Lookout Peak. To the east, through the trees, you can see the peaks of the Great

Western Divide. Behind you, to the south, is Big Baldy (Walk No. 16).

After you've enjoyed this 90-degree view, retrace your steps to your car.

18 Lost Grove

This easy .5-mile Walk, just off the Generals Highway, takes you quickly to several clusters of giant sequoia trees.

The Walk is just inside the northwest boundary of Sequoia National Park. It begins in a parking area on the Generals Highway 11 miles northwest of the park's Lodgepole Visitor Center and about two miles southeast of Stony Creek Village in Sequoia National Forest. The Generals Highway conveniently runs through one of the densest concentrations of mature sequoias in Lost Grove so you'll see many of the giants even before you begin your Walk.

Park on either side of the highway and take the paved path that climbs up the slope on the east side of the road. In about 300 feet the path loops around a giant sequoia that's about 30 feet wide at its base. You'll see several other sequoias here too.

Now follow the paved path back to the highway and cross the road. Near the restrooms (which are faced with sequoia bark) you'll see an unpaved path marked by signs saying "North Park Boundary" and "Dorst Campground." Follow the path, which heads to the right, down the slope, away from the restrooms and parallel to the highway. In about 50 feet you'll come to an unmarked trail junction. Go straight ahead. The trail then switches back and forth down to a small, usually dry creek at the bottom of the slope, about .2 miles from the restrooms. Here you'll find another cluster of big sequoias.

You've now seen the densest collection of giant sequoias in the grove, which means you've seen the most big trees in the area for the least effort. If you walk farther, you will find mature sequoias fewer and farther between. We therefore suggest you turn around here and retrace your steps to your car. If you want to see more large sequoias, take Walk No. 1, in Grant Grove, or Walks No. 23, 24 and 29, in the Giant Forest.

19 Little Baldy

This moderate 3.5-mile round trip takes you to the top of a 8,044-foot granite dome with one of the best panoramic views in the parks. You'll see the Silliman Crest, the Tableland, Castle Rocks, Sunset and Moro rocks, the Great Western Divide and the canyons of four rivers: the Marble, Middle, East and South forks of the Kaweah River. On your way to the top you'll also have views of Big Baldy and Chimney Rock.

The Walk is in Sequoia National Park. The trailhead is on a high point in the Generals Highway, known as the Little Baldy Saddle, about 6.8 miles west of the Lodgepole Visitor Center. The trail begins on the north side of the road. It's marked by a brown-stained sign with incised yellow letters.

The trail goes up steps, into a grove of fir trees. Then it climbs steeply but briefly as it switches back to the right, then to the left before it begins a long, gentle climb up the steep lower slope of Little Baldy.

After about .4 miles you can begin to see, on your left, the bare rock of 8,209-foot Big Baldy (Walk No. 16) on a ridge about five miles to the northwest. In front of Big Baldy is 7,711-foot Chimney Rock, a rock turret that really does resemble a chimney. You'll have all but continuous views of both promontories as you climb along the shelf carved into the slope of Little Baldy.

After about .8 miles the trail switches back to the right, evergreen trees are gradually supplanted by oaks, manzanita bushes and grasses, and the views become even wider. On a clear day you can see the San Joaquin Valley to the west and the foothills to the southwest.

Soon the trail switches back to the left again, then to the right, as it traverses an ever more open and grassy slope.

About halfway to the summit, the path levels out and rolls gently through evergreen woods and large drifts of lupine for about a mile. Between the trees you have occasional views of the bare Tableland and the Silliman Crest to the east and Castle Rocks and the canyon of the Middle Fork of the Kaweah River to the south.

Finally the trail makes a steep but very brief climb to the top of Little Baldy. From its nearly flat, bare,

120-foot-long, 60-foot-wide granite summit you have panoramic views. You can see the Silliman Crest, in the northeast; the Tableland and the Kings Kaweah Divide, in the east; and the Great Western Divide, in the east and southeast — all bare, creased, pointed and often snowcapped two-mile-high peaks. In the southeast, just three miles away, is the canyon of the Marble Fork of the Kaweah River and the outcrop of 6,412-foot Sunset Rock (Walk No. 25), on the southeastern slope of the canyon. Beyond the Marble Fork is the canyon of the Middle Fork of the Kaweah. On the southern slope of the canyon and directly beyond Sunset Rock are the 9,081-foot Castle Rocks. Peeking above the north slope of the Middle Fork canyon, in the south-southeast, is the bare, rounded top of 6,725-foot Moro Rock (Walk No. 28). Farther to the southeast are the canyons of the East and South forks of the Kaweah, as well as layers of long, forested ridges between the canyons. To the south and west are dry, nearly treeless, grass- and yucca-covered foothills: the 5,612-foot Ash Peaks to the south-southwest and 4,927-foot Yucca Mountain to the southwest. Just a couple of miles to the west is Pine Ridge. Much farther to the west is the smoggy San Joaquin Valley. To the northwest are Chimney Rock and Big Baldy.

Take time to enjoy this panorama, perhaps over refreshments or a picnic lunch. When you're ready, follow the trail back to your car.

20 Tokopah Falls

This moderate 3.4-mile round trip takes you

up the Marble Fork of the Kaweah River into the glacier-carved, half-mile-deep Tokopah Valley. You'll have often continuous views of the Watchtower rising 1,600 feet above you and you'll see Tokopah Falls cascade more than 100 feet down the steep headwalls of the valley.

The Walk begins about .6 miles east of the Lodgepole Visitor Center in Sequoia National Park. To reach the trailhead, follow the paved road past the visitor center, into Lodgepole Campground. About .5 miles from the visitor center you'll see the Lodgepole Nature Center on your right and, just after the nature center, a wide bridge over the Marble Fork, on your left. Park on the left side of the road, walk across the bridge and note the boulders and wide pools in the rock-bottomed river. On the other side of the bridge, on your right, you'll see the trail to Tokopah Falls. Upstream you'll see the steep rock walls of Tokopah Valley.

The wide, well-worn, sandy path follows the Marble Fork upriver. As you pass scattered firs and other evergreens you'll have almost constant views, on your right, of the 40- to 50-foot-wide river, which in the summer seems to have more rocks than water in it. You'll also see tents in the campground on the other side of the stream and through the trees you'll catch glimpses of the valley's clifflike walls. The Watchtower (Walk No. 21), the glacier-polished rock promontory that looms 1,600 feet above the valley, will gradually come into view and you'll be able to see this landmark throughout most of the rest of the Walk.

Less than .5 miles from the trailhead you'll leave the campground behind and the path will run briefly away from the river and through thicker evergreen woods. Then it will return to the Marble Fork, where you'll see it surge down a narrow sluiceway into large pools.

After crossing a wide, wet meadow on causeways bordered with stones, the path splits. Take the left fork, which quickly climbs to the top of a ledgy overlook, from which you can see the river flowing over wide ledges.

Next the path crosses several dry branches of a tiny creek that flows into the Marble Fork. Then it splits again. As before, take the left fork to the top of an overlook, where you'll have another view of the Marble Fork flowing smoothly over ledges.

About 1.5 miles from the trailhead you'll cross several branches of Horse Creek, which runs into the Marble Fork. You'll cross the tiny streamlets on stones or on wooden bridges made either of planks or half-logs. You're now abreast of and just a few hundred feet from the base of the Watchtower, on the other side of the Marble Fork.

Soon the woods beside the trail get rockier and all of a sudden there are no more evergreens at all — just oaks, deciduous bushes and wildflowers. You're now entering the horseshoe-shaped cirque at the head of Tokopah Valley and you're surrounded on three sides by rock walls almost half a mile high. Ahead of you is Tokopah Falls, cascading down the steep sides of the cirque.

The now sunny path climbs gently over, under and between the boulders of a talus slope. Many of the enormous, sharp-edged rocks look as if they were freshly broken. That's because the Civilian Conservation Corps used dynamite to blast the trail through the rocks in the 1930s.

About 1.7 miles from the trailhead, the path ends abruptly at the base of the cirque, just a couple of hundred feet from the rocky base of the falls. You can't see the top of the falls from here but you have a good view of the bottom. At the top of the ledge the falls split into two streams, each of which cascades, trickles and splatters about 50 feet down the rough, wide rock. Then the two streams come together and slide another 50 feet down a flume in the ledge before plunging into a 25-foot-square pool at the base of the falls.

The head of Tokopah Valley is a stunning, alpinelike setting, a treeless world of gray rock and water. Fat, short-legged marmots waddle around and a few pikas, about the size of small squirrels, dart along the stony ledges. This is a fine place for a picnic or at least a long pause before turning around and walking back to your car.

21 The Watchtower

This moderately strenuous 9.2-mile round trip offers stunning continuous clifftop views of the Marble Fork canyon, Tokopah Valley and the slopes of the vast creased rock amphitheater known as the Tableland. The Walk also brings you to the charming, rock-bound Heather

Both this Walk and Walk No. 22 are more taxing than other Great Walks. Both climb about 1,800 feet in about 4.6 miles and sometimes the climbing is a bit steep. That doesn't mean you shouldn't take the Walk — like any Great Walk, it shouldn't be missed. But it does mean that you should make the Walk as comfortable as possible by walking slowly and pausing often. Also note that you can't take this Walk in the winter or early spring because the trail to the Watchtower is closed because of ice and snow.

The Walk begins in the Wolverton section of Sequoia National Park. To reach the trailhead, turn off the Generals Highway onto the Wolverton road about 1.5 miles south of the Lodgepole Visitor Center and about two miles north of Giant Forest Lodge. The Wolverton road almost immediately passes the road to the Wolverton Corrals, on the right, and, about 1.5 miles from the Generals Highway, arrives at a large parking area, where you take your first left. The trail begins at a set of concrete steps on the left (north) side of the parking area, about 200 feet from the Wolverton road.

The smooth path, known as the Lakes Trail, im-

A walker gazes at Ed by Ned, two giant sequoias fused together at their bases, near the beginning of the trail to **Sunset Rock** *(Walk No. 25).*

▶

mediately climbs through fir trees. In about 300 feet the Long Meadow Loop Trail runs into the Lakes Trail on the left. Take a right at this intersection. Just a few yards ahead, the Long Meadow Loop Trail leaves the Lakes Trail on the right. Take a left here.

The Lakes Trail now climbs gently along the south rim of the canyon of the Marble Fork of the Kaweah River. The path often runs along the spines of lateral moraines, which are long, stony ridges deposited by a glacier. These moraines were left by the Tokopah Glacier, which carved the 800-foot-deep canyon to your left. Through the trees on your left you have almost constant views of the forested north slopes of the canyon and the bare, pointed ledges above it.

In about .7 miles the trail levels off and you'll start to hear, but not quite see, Wolverton Creek flowing softly on your right. Then the views of the canyon disappear as the trail runs along the side of a low ridge, on your left, and beside a wet, shady meadow, on your right, beside Wolverton Creek. Handsome chinquapin bushes and evergreens covered with green staghorn lichen grow on both sides of the path.

In about a mile the trail turns right, away from the Marble Fork canyon, and climbs along a slope that rises above Wolverton Creek. The path runs in and out of evergreen woods and crosses a half-dozen tiny meadows filled with asters, lupines and other wildflowers.

At the eastern end of the last meadow the trail crosses a trickling creek filled with wildflowers, then climbs through more evergreens and, about 1.8 miles from the trailhead, reaches a junction. The

Alta Trail to Panther Gap (Walk No. 22) goes to the right, the Lakes Trail to the left.

Follow the Lakes Trail as it keeps climbing through the evergreen forest. About .1 miles from the trail junction you'll recross the creek, here filled with flowers and ferns, that you crossed .2 miles before.

In another .1 miles the trail forks again. Both paths take you to Heather Lake but the right fork has two drawbacks: It's very steep—it goes over a ridge appropriately named "The Hump"—and it bypasses the Watchtower. The left fork takes you to both Heather Lake and the Watchtower and by a much gentler route. The last time we were here someone had scratched the word "muscles" under the arrow pointing to the Hump trail and the word "brains" under the arrow pointing to the Watchtower trail. *Touché!*

Take the "brains" route, which immediately becomes more moderate and soon provides views, through the trees on your left, of the steep, glacier-polished rock walls of Tokopah Valley (Walk No. 20), in the upper Middle Fork canyon.

Next you'll cross a lush, long, 50-foot-wide strip meadow filled with ferns, lupine and other wildflowers. The meadow is watered by a tiny creek—a tributary of the Middle Fork—that you cross on stones.

As you climb closer to the top of the Watchtower, the trail traverses an ever steeper slope and brings you closer and closer to Tokopah Valley. Your views, through the trees, of the evergreen-dotted canyon walls and the bare rock peaks beyond them get better and better. Soon you'll be able to see deep

into the Marble Fork canyon and you'll also have your first views of the light gray outcrop of the Watchtower looming ahead of you.

Then the trail switches back to the right, then to the left before it climbs through open evergreen woods to a ledge on the left of the trail, on the rim of Tokopah Valley. Walk slowly and carefully to the edge of the ledge. With each step you'll see another 100 feet farther into the 1,500-foot-deep canyon in front of you. When you reach the edge of the canyon you'll see the nose of the Watchtower, on your left, which extends both up and out, into the canyon, then plunges almost straight down, hundreds of feet, to the bottom of the valley. Barely visible at the very bottom of the Watchtower is the end of the Tokopah Falls trail (Walk No. 20) and the base of Tokopah Falls. To the left and right of the Watchtower you can see deep into the awesome, wrinkled rock canyon. To your right, above Tokopah Valley, is a vast creased rock amphitheater—the lower slopes of the Tableland. It's a world that seems to be made only of bare ledge, on which, somehow, a few scraggly evergreens and other plants manage surrealistically to grow. This sweeping bowl both awes you with its scale and fascinates you with its complex, delicate crinkles and tiny cracks. Look carefully and you can see the dark gray bed of a tiny tributary of the Marble Fork trickling across the ledge.

A child is fascinated by a cluster of mature sequoias in **Lost Grove** *(Walk No. 18), near the Generals Highway.*
◄

This is arguably the most moving canyon view in the parks. And the vista continues as the trail climbs briefly up the slope of the canyon and then follows a gently graded shelf blasted into the nearly vertical canyon walls. (The trail is wide and perfectly safe but it *is* on the edge of the cliff. If that makes you nervous, you may want to turn around here.) These clifflike slopes will be the steepest ones you'll traverse on the entire Walk. The trail is now a corniche, a dramatic linear observation platform from which you'll have continuous 180-degree views up and down the canyon. You'll see the trail to Tokopah Falls, almost 2,000 feet below you, and the Watchtower behind you.

About .3 miles from the Watchtower, the trail curves to the right and rounds a corner of the cliff. Now you'll see more of the immense rock bowl that is the source of the Marble Fork. So barren is this ledge that even its floor, where you might expect to find at least a little soil, is as bare as the rest of the rock.

Next the trail climbs slightly, then starts descending gradually until, about .7 miles from the Watchtower, the Hump trail rejoins the Watchtower trail.

Go straight ahead and follow the nearly level path through sparse lodgepole pines until, in about .1 miles, you come to Heather Lake, a 300-foot-wide tarn tucked against steep rock walls. The rocky north side of the lake has thick patches of red-blooming heather and tiny ledges that make fine picnic spots. There's also a ledge island on the west side of the lake that, if the water is low enough, can be reached by walking across grass and logs.

The last time we were here — an overcast, early

September day—clouds would blow in like white smoke and quickly blanket the lake, hiding everything except the rocky shore in front of us. Then the clouds would suddenly disappear and the entire emerald green lake would reemerge.

The cloud show continued after we turned around and started to follow the trail back to our car. Long trains of white clouds, most of them at eye level, would drift up the canyon past the Watchtower and quickly fill the amphitheater, now on our right, so that we could see only the ledge shelf at our feet and the cliff on our left. After a few minutes, the clouds would leave as quickly as they came in, dramatically opening up the wide views to our right.

If you'd like to see a bit farther up the Tableland and don't mind a very steep but very brief climb to get to the view, walk about 600 feet up the Hump trail. In that distance you'll climb about 300 feet—a rate of about 2,600 feet per mile—about as steep as trails get. You'll quickly come to the top of the ridge known as the Hump and you'll be able to see some of the more-than-two-mile-high peaks that form the divide between Sequoia and Kings Canyon national parks. After you've enjoyed the vista, return to the Watchtower trail and savor its views again as you walk back to your car.

22 Panther Gap

This moderately strenuous eight-mile round trip offers almost two miles of grand and nearly

continuous views from an open trail on the edge of the canyon of the Middle Fork of the Kaweah River. Your vistas will include Moro Rock, Castle Rocks, Panther Peak, Tharp's Rock, Sugarbowl Dome, Tokopah Valley and the bare, pointed peaks of the Great Western Divide.

The first 1.8 miles of this Walk follow the route of the Watchtower trail (Walk No. 21). See page 95 for a description of that Walk as well as directions to the trailhead. If you don't want to walk the same route twice or if you're short of time, you might want to ride a horse or mule over the route of Walk No. 21 and do only the remainder of this Walk on foot. Check with the Wolverton Corrals (at 209-565-3445) to see if they have horses or mules available, as well as a wrangler to ride with you and lead your mounts back to the corrals.

At the intersection 1.8 miles from the trailhead take a right onto the Alta Trail and climb gently toward Panther Gap. The trail parallels Wolverton Creek and you'll occasionally hear, but never quite see, the creek on your right. You will, however, cross several tiny tributaries of the creek, as well as several sunny meadows thick with grasses, ferns and wildflowers.

The sharp peaks of the Great Western Divide seen on the trail from **Panther Gap** *(Walk No. 22), on the edge of the canyon of the Middle Fork of the Kaweah River.*
◀

About 2.7 miles from the trailhead you'll see the steep slope of a ridge stretching across the trail in front of you. The top of the ridge is Panther Gap. The trail climbs up to the gap by switching back and forth through open evergreen woods. When you reach the gap, in another .1 miles, you'll be 8,400 feet high and on the edge of the Middle Fork canyon. Here you'll have spectacular views in almost every direction.

Ahead, on the south slope of the canyon, are the 9,081-foot Castle Rocks. Below you are the canyon's sharply creased, forested walls. Eight miles to your left are the bare, pointed, purple and gray summits of the Great Western Divide. When we were here last—a sunny late August day—the peaks were still flecked with snow. To your right are the oak- and grass-covered foothills of the Sierra, the receding ridges between the forks of the Kaweah, and the low, haze-covered plain of the San Joaquin Valley. Behind you is the bare, steep north slope of Tokopah Valley (Walk No. 20).

After you've absorbed these remarkable views, follow the smooth, sandy Alta Trail to the left. You'll immediately climb up the north side of the ridge to the east of Panther Gap and you'll soon see a solitary stone pinnacle on the steep slope of the canyon, behind you. To your left you'll have more views of the north wall of Tokopah Valley.

Then the trail climbs around to the south side of the ridge—toward the Middle Fork canyon—and levels off. Now you'll have views, partly through the trees, of Castle Rocks, the Great Western Divide and Panther Peak, a 9,046-foot-high point on the steep ridge west of Panther Gap, behind you.

Then the trees all but disappear and for almost another mile you'll have uninterrupted views up and down the canyon as the trail follows a shelf carved into the steep rim of the valley. You'll pass manzanita, chinquapin and ceanothus bushes as the sunny trail gently and often imperceptibly climbs up the open slope. This part of the Walk is one of the most exhilarating in the parks.

Soon you'll have views back to Moro Rock (Walk No. 28) as well as of ragged rocks and spires both above and below the trail. You'll also pass wildflower-filled hanging gardens, so called because they grow in the moist ravines of creeks flowing down the steep slope, so they look as if they're "hanging" on the canyon walls.

About 3.7 miles from the trailhead you'll come to another intersection. The Seven Mile Hill Trail goes to the right, down the canyon, to the High Sierra Trail (Walk No. 42). Stay on the Alta Trail, which goes straight ahead.

Now you have a 270-degree view. On your far left is Tharp's Rock, a pointed, 10,500-foot rock promontory visible through the trees. Ahead of you is the 7,875-foot Sugarbowl Dome. Beyond the dome is the Great Western Divide. Across the canyon are Castle Rocks and on your far right are Moro Rock and Panther Peak.

In another .1 miles there's still another good view of the Great Western Divide and, about .2 miles after that, the trail curves down to tree-shaded Mehrten Creek, which you cross on stones. On the other side of the small creek are several camp sites. A few feet downstream is the 300-foot-square Mehrten

Meadow, which is filled with Bigelow's sneezeweed, Queen Anne's lace, Indian paintbrush, wild onions, lavender phlox, lupine and other wildflowers. It's a pleasant spot for a rest before you turn around and follow the trail back to Wolverton — and enjoy some of the best views in the parks all over again.

23 Congress Trail

You'll see dozens of giant sequoias in a relatively short time and for relatively little effort on this easy 2.3-mile loop. You'll see the General Sherman Tree, the world's largest living thing, and the House, Senate and Founders groups, three unusually dense clusters of mature sequoias. A 22-page trail guide describes the named sequoias along the route and explains how these trees manage to live to be thousands of years old.

The Walk is in the Giant Forest, in Sequoia National Park. It begins in a parking area just off the Generals Highway, about 1.5 miles north of the Giant Forest Lodge and about two miles south of the Lodgepole Visitor Center. Turn north off the Gen-

A black bear hunts for his dinner in the **Giant Forest** *(Walks No. 23–30).*
◄

erals Highways at a sign saying "Sherman Tree." The paved road goes quickly uphill into a parking loop, less than a couple of hundred feet from the Sherman Tree. (If the loop is full you can park in the lot along the Generals Highway.)

On the edge of the parking loop, beside the path to the Sherman Tree, is a mounted 16-foot-wide cross-section of a 2,400-year-old sequoia.

Cross the road on which you drove to the parking loop and follow the paved path that takes you around the Sherman Tree. The Sherman is a bundle of superlatives: not just the largest sequoia in the world, or the largest tree in the world, but the largest living organism on earth. As a sign in front of the tree explains, while other trees are taller or thicker, "no other living thing on this planet exceeds the volume of this giant sequoia." According to the Park Service, the Sherman Tree is between 2,300 and 2,700 years old, more than 274 feet tall—higher than a 27-story building—more than 36 feet thick and more than 102 feet around at its base. Its largest *branch* is bigger than most *trees* east of the Mississippi River.

After you've contemplated the Sherman Tree, pick up a copy of the *Congress Trail* guide, which is for sale in a box near the tree. The pamphlet, which is keyed to numbered stops along the Congress Trail, tells the fascinating story of how sequoias long outlive all their forest rivals.

Now follow the paved path back to the road leading to the parking loop. After you reach the road, walk along the paved path beside the split-rail fence on the north side of the road, as if you were going back to your car. Less than 200 feet from the Sherman Tree you'll see a brown sign with yellow letters indicating where the four-foot-wide asphalt Congress Trail heads to the left, into a forest of sugar pines, white firs and, of course, sequoias.

The wide, smooth path quickly comes to the Leaning Tree, a giant sequoia that does just that. As the trail guide explains, leaning sequoias like this one try to stop themselves from falling over by growing bigger, heavier branches on the side opposite the direction they're leaning.

The trail immediately crosses tiny Sherman Creek, then very gradually climbs the slope above the wide swale to the right of the path. During the next .3 miles you'll cross two more tiny creeks, both of which flow into Sherman Creek, on your right. Sequoias along this part of the trail help illustrate what the trail guide explains: how the sequoia's resin-free, two-foot-thick bark protects the tree from forest fires and, paradoxically, how sequoias *need* fires to propagate the species.

About .4 miles from the trailhead you'll reach a trail junction. The short path on the right goes to the western leg of the loop trail, which you can see below you, on the right. Later you'll follow that part of the trail back to your car. Right now walk straight ahead. You'll soon pass several sequoias with large, dramatic fire scars. As the trail guide explains, sequoias "heal" these scars by completely covering them with new growth.

In about .8 miles you'll come to a four-way junction. The Trail of the Sequoias goes straight ahead, the Alta Trail goes both left and right. Stay on the Congress Trail, which follows the Alta Trail to the right for a few hundred feet, then leaves the Alta Trail on the left.

About .1 miles from the Alta Trail, the Congress Trail reaches the President Tree, which, according to the trail guide, is the fourth-largest giant sequoia in the world. The tree was dedicated to the memory of President Warren G. Harding in 1923, the year he died in office. Parts of the base of the tree resemble flying buttresses and a 25-foot-high fire scar in its base looks like a sculpture niche.

Just beyond the President Tree a trail on the left takes you, in just a couple of hundred feet, to the Chief Sequoyah Tree, named after the learned Cherokee Indian who created a syllabary, or phonetic alphabet, for his tribe. Whether the sequoia species is also named after Sequoyah is, as the trail guide says, uncertain.

Return to the Congress Trail and in about .1 miles you'll come to the Senate Group, an impressive cluster of about a dozen giant sequoias in a larger group of about 50 trees. Some of the big trees are barely a yard apart. Standing beneath so many massive trees is an awesome experience.

The trail now passes through ferns and lupines, curves by the 20-foot-high roots of a fallen sequoia, skirts the northern edge of Circle Meadow, on the left, and, just a few hundred feet from the Senate Group, comes to the House Group, another impres-

The General Sherman Tree, the world's largest living thing, near the beginning of the **Congress Trail** *(Walk No. 23).*
▶

sive collection of a dozen or so giant sequoias. Like the Senate Group, many trees in the House Group are barely a yard apart and the entire cluster fills an area about 50 feet square. The stand looks like a wall of sequoias, or a giant hedge. When you consider how thick the trees are — about 12 feet — it's apparent that sequoias grow closer together, relative to their mass, than almost any other tree. If sugar pines, for example, were to grow as close, relative to their size, they would be only inches apart; they would create an almost solid mass of wood on the forest floor. If you want to look at the House Group at length you can do so in the comfort of one of two old sequoia benches beside the trail.

Next you'll pass some severely fire-scarred trees, on the left, and, just a few hundred feet from the House Group, you'll come to another giant sequoia, the 250-foot-tall, 25-foot-wide General Lee Tree, named after the Confederate commander.

Immediately after the General Lee Tree the Congress Trail intersects the Alta Trail again. Take a left on the Alta Trail, pass the McKinley Tree, on the right (you'll come back to it in a few minutes), and almost immediately make another left onto another, unnamed trail. Follow it until, in less than 100 feet, you come to the Room Tree. Inside this suitably named sequoia is a six-by-nine-foot-wide, 30-foot-high "room" complete with a 12-foot-high "window," all of which were hollowed out of the tree by fire.

Another 100 feet down the trail is a third dense cluster of about a dozen giant sequoias. This is the Founders Group. According to a sign here the trees are "dedicated to those men who contributed so much toward the establishment of this park."

Now go back to the Alta Trail, *cross* the trail and almost immediately take a left onto the paved spur trail that leads away from the McKinley Tree. At the end of this 100-foot-long trail you can see all of the 241-foot-tall, 28-foot-wide McKinley Tree, named for President William McKinley after he was assassinated in 1901.

Walk back to the McKinley Tree, take a left and you'll immediately be back on the paved Congress Trail. Soon you'll come to a fallen sequoia on your right that is reportedly used by bears as a winter den. To find the den, walk along the left side of the tree and look underneath.

The trail next comes to the top of a slope that drops steeply to your left. You'll see the Generals Highway below and mountain ridges in the distance.

As the trail gradually descends the slope on its way back to the parking loop, now less than .7 miles away, you'll pass more mature sequoias, including several with dramatic fire scars. You'll also walk under one fallen tree that, according to the trail guide, "fell at about 9:15 on the clear, windless evening of June 25, 1965. Rangers on duty two miles away heard the tremendous roar and knew that a giant had fallen." Today the tree remains where it fell — across the trail. A four-foot-wide, six-foot-high tunnel was cut in the bottom of the massive tree so people could walk underneath it.

24 Hazelwood Nature Trail

This easy one-mile loop takes you past many large sequoias in a lush grove, and interesting signs along the trail describe some special characteristics of these giant trees.

The Walk begins at a small parking area on the Generals Highway opposite the Giant Forest Lodge in Sequoia National Park.

You'll barely start walking when you'll pass between two mature sequoias and go by a large drift of lupine on your right. Then you'll walk by a fallen sequoia, one of many you'll see on the Walk, and immediately go *through* another fallen sequoia by walking across a four-foot-wide, seven-foot-deep notch cut into the tree. Next you'll skirt a small, sunny meadow filled with ferns, on your right. Then you'll climb over a tiny ridge into a moist swale thick with sequoias, firs and even a few dogwoods. The green staghorn lichen grows so thick in this wet grove that it covers almost the entire bark of some firs and makes the trees themselves look green. A few feet ahead is a trail junction. The trail on the left is the end of the Hazelwood Nature Trail loop. Go right and follow the trail counterclockwise along the bottom of the ridge to your right.

About .4 miles from the trailhead the path splits

again. The Soldiers Trail goes to the right, the nature trail to the left. Take a left.

About .7 miles from the trailhead the path curves close to the Generals Highway and forks again. Go left again. Soon you'll cross a bridge over a tiny, trickling creek that's thick with wildflowers and grasses. Then you'll come to another junction. Make yet another left and almost immediately you'll come to the end of the nature trail loop. Take a right here and retrace your steps to the trailhead.

25 Sunset Rock

This easy, pleasant two-mile round trip takes you to 6,412-foot Sunset Rock, where you'll have views up and down the canyon of the Marble Fork of the Kaweah River. En route you'll pass two small meadows and many giant sequoias.

The Walk begins in the paved parking lot beside Round Meadow, in Sequoia National Park. To reach the trailhead turn off the Generals Highway just a couple of hundred feet west of Giant Forest Lodge and about .2 miles east of Giant Forest Village. In about 300 feet you'll reach the paved parking area, which is surrounded by large sequoias. The trail begins on the west side of the parking area, about 50 feet south of two huge sequoias (known as Ed by Ned) that are joined together at their bases. If you plan to watch the sunset from the rock, bring a flashlight so you can see the path on your way back to your car.

About 30 feet up the paved path you'll see an incised wood sign saying that Sunset Rock is one mile ahead.

About 100 feet after the sign the path splits. The paved trail to the left goes to Giant Forest Village. Take the unpaved path on your right and you'll immediately be in front of the Clara Barton Tree, one of a very few sequoias named after women. The 20-foot-thick tree is surrounded by many other sequoias, large and small.

Now the path skirts a tiny meadow, on the left, and follows tiny Little Deer Creek, also on the left, through an open woods of sequoias, firs, incense-cedars and chinquapin bushes.

About .3 miles from the trailhead, you'll reach another junction. The trail on the left crosses Little Deer Creek on a wooden bridge and goes on to Giant Forest Village. The trail to Sunset Rock goes straight ahead. It gradually curves away from the creek and climbs almost imperceptibly to the top of a grade that slopes to the left, toward Little Deer Creek and, beyond the creek, toward the Marble Fork of the Kaweah River. Through the trees on your left you'll see the opposite (west) side of the Marble Fork canyon.

About .5 miles from the trailhead you'll cross the western edge of a 100-foot-wide meadow known as Eli's Paradise. Near the other side of the meadow is an enormous boulder, about 20 feet wide and 20 feet high, that rests all by itself in the thick grass.

You're now near the northern edge of the Giant

Forest Grove and the sequoias soon disappear. They're replaced by an often sunny, almost parklike woods of firs, incense-cedars and other evergreens.

As you walk easily along the often ledgy edge of the canyon, you'll begin to have continuous views, sometimes through trees, of the Marble Fork canyon, on your left. To your rear you'll see the foothills in the south. On the horizon, on the west side of the canyon, you'll see the low granite dome of 8,044-foot Little Baldy (Walk No. 19).

About a mile from the trailhead the path forks again. The trail on the right goes to the Marble Fork Bridge. The path on the left takes you immediately onto Sunset Rock, a nearly level, 200-foot-wide ledge at the edge of the Marble Fork canyon. Ahead of you is Little Baldy. To your left are the 5,612-foot Ash Peaks and other foothills to the south. To your right is the bare, two-mile-high Silliman Crest.

After you've enjoyed the view, retrace your steps to your car.

26 Beetle Rock

This 700-foot round trip takes you to a broad, rolling ledge where you have a wide view across the Marble Fork canyon. If you're looking for a quick- and easy-to-get-to spot to watch the sunset, this is it.

Beetle Rock is at the edge of Giant Forest Village, in Sequoia National Park. To get there, leave your

car at the village parking area and start walking south along the Generals Highway. (Bring a flashlight if you plan to watch the sunset and walk back after dark.) You'll immediately come to a road on your right that leads to the motels and cabins in the Kaweah Area of the Giant Forest Lodge (you can see the motels from the village). Follow that road for just about 30 feet and you'll see, on your left, a four-foot-wide asphalt path marked by a sign saying "Beetle Rock Center." Follow the walkway, which passes sequoias and other large evergreen trees. In only about 300 feet you'll come to Beetle Rock Center, a big, brown, rustic-looking building used for large gatherings. Just to the right of the building is Beetle Rock, a several-hundred-foot-wide, light gray granite outcrop at the edge of the forested Marble Fork canyon. The view from here is similar to that from Sunset Rock (Walk No. 25), except that you have closer views of the Ash Peaks and the foothills to your left. Ahead of you are rolling layers of hills and far to your right is the low, bare dome of Little Baldy (Walk No. 19).

27 Hanging Rock

This undemanding .2-mile round trip takes you to two overlooks on the edge of the canyon

---

The Senate Group of giant sequoias on the **Congress Trail** *(Walk No. 23).*
◀

of the Middle Fork of the Kaweah River. You'll see the remarkable Hanging Rock, you'll have a very close view of Moro Rock and you'll see the Middle Fork River, half-a-mile below, and the layers of foothills beyond it.

The Walk is on the southern edge of the Giant Forest Grove in Sequoia National Park. To get to the trailhead, turn off the Generals Highway and onto the Crescent Meadow Road in Giant Forest Village. About a mile from the village the road forks. Take a right onto the one-way loop road to Moro Rock (Walk No. 28). About .1 miles from the intersection you'll come to a parking turnout on the right. A trail sign here says Hanging Rock is .1 miles away. (From here you can sometimes see cars parked in front of Moro Rock, which is just a few hundred feet away.)

The path climbs steeply but very briefly through the shady sequoia forest and quickly brings you to an overlook on the rim of the Marble Fork canyon, on the left of the trail. Here you can see the west side of Moro Rock, which is more than 1,000 feet from top to bottom. From this vantage point it looks like an enormous gray rock fin. Look carefully and you'll probably see people on the top. Here, too, you'll get your first glimpse into the Marble Fork canyon — a taste of the view to come.

Keep walking up the smooth trail. After a steep but very short climb the path emerges onto a sunlit rock outcrop on the rim of the canyon. The 200-foot-long gray ledge is surrounded on three sides by pungent carpets of mountain misery and by thick, handsome drifts of manzanita bushes. The south side of the ledge slopes toward the canyon, then drops precipitously. (There's no railing here. Be careful.) Near the middle of this sloping ledge is Hanging Rock, a 20-foot-wide, seven-foot-high boulder shaped like a flying saucer. The well-named solitary rock seems to be just . . . well, hanging on the ledge, defying the laws of gravity as it refuses to simply slide off the outcrop into the canyon.

The attraction here, however, is not just Hanging Rock but also the view beyond it: the Middle Fork Canyon, in some places almost a mile deep; the rapids of the Middle Fork, half a mile below you; the Generals Highway switching back and forth up the steep slope of the canyon and the four-mile-long, one-mile-high Ash Peaks Ridge, on your right, to the southwest. On a clear day you'll see at least five layers of ridges, each a lighter shade of blue than the one in front of it.

After you've enjoyed this unique overlook, follow the path back to your car.

28 Moro Rock

This remarkable and undemanding .6-mile round trip is the most exciting short Great Walk in the parks. The trail doesn't take you *to* an overlook. Rather, the trail is almost entirely *on* an overlook: 6,725-foot Moro Rock, which slightly resembles an enormous, 1,000-foot egg standing on end on the rim of the Marble Fork

canyon. Nearly 400 steps take you smoothly up the spine of the rock to the top. You'll have constant views and they'll be in all directions — from the Great Western Divide in the east, to the Middle Fork canyon in the south and west, to the Giant Forest Grove to the north. Plaques along the trail describe the vistas. What's more, Moro Rock is the best place in the Giant Forest to watch sunrises and sunsets.

The Walk is steep — it climbs 300 feet in .3 miles, a rate of 1,000 feet per mile. But the Walk is short, the steps and ramps are well made (see below) and handrails make the climb easier. We suggest you climb slowly, both to make the Walk easier and to give you time to appreciate the world-class views. If you plan to watch the sunset, bring along a flashlight to use on your way back.

Like Hanging Rock (Walk No. 27), this Walk is on the southern edge of the Giant Forest Grove, in Sequoia National Park. To get to the trailhead, turn off the Generals Highway and onto the Crescent Meadow Road in Giant Forest Village. About a mile from the village the road forks. Take a right onto the one-way loop road to Moro Rock. About .2 miles from the intersection you'll come to a parking area in

The House Group of giant sequoias on the **Congress Trail** *(Walk No. 23).*
◄

front of the rock, which rises in front of you like a little Gibraltar on the edge of the Marble Fork canyon.

A sign here explains that the stone-and-concrete steps going up the rock were built in 1931 and that, because of their "sensitive design" and the "craftsmanship" with which they were built, they were entered in the National Register of Historic Places in 1978. The sign also says that "no one knows the origin" of the rock's name but that there are other places named "Moro" or "Morro" in California, New Mexico and Puerto Rico—all present or former Spanish-speaking areas—and that *moro* is a Spanish word for "promontory."

The path immediately takes you onto the rock. From here to the top the path will be unlike any other Great Walk in the parks—or almost anywhere else, for that matter. It will be not on dirt but entirely on what landscape designers call hardscape: manmade concrete steps, ramps and landings, and, of course, Moro Rock itself. As the path climbs the rock it switches from one side of it to the other, giving you views both up and down the canyon. It also pauses at many landings and each one offers such an outstanding view that Moro Rock would be a Great Walk even if it had just one of them.

You'll quickly see the Great Western Divide and a plaque on the left of the path identifies its summits, including the 12,634-foot Triple Divide Peak, the highest mountain you can see at this point, and six other peaks that are more than 12,000 feet high. On the other side of the canyon are the towers and spires of 9,081-foot Castle Rocks.

Soon you'll be able to see, to the right of the path, the Generals Highway zigzagging up the steep north slope of the canyon. Beyond the highway, in the distance, are a half-dozen nearly parallel ridges, one behind the other, each one slightly paler than the one in front of it. Every one of these ridges seems to begin from one point near the top of the cliff at the edge of the canyon to your right and each one seems to slope gradually downward to the left.

Next you'll come to a plaque that explains that the Middle Fork canyon is almost as deep as the Grand Canyon, in Arizona, that the top of Moro Rock is 4,000 feet higher than the floor of the Middle Fork canyon in front of it and that other parts of the canyon are even deeper.

Another plaque explains how altitude affects climate and how climate, in turn, affects vegetation — that the foothills to the southwest receive only a little rain and snow, so they can grow only grasses, brush and small oaks, but that land above 5,000 feet, such as the Giant Forest Grove, gets a lot of precipitation — mainly winter snow — and can therefore produce dense forests of large, water-loving conifers. On the other hand, the plaque continues, the climate above 9,000 feet is so severe that even conifers no longer do well; above 12,000 feet, where the ground is covered with ice and snow much of the year, trees "disappear entirely."

Yet another plaque says that on a clear day you can see the Coast Range, 100 miles away, but that because of increasing air pollution clear days are rare.

At the end of the trail at the top of the rock,

swallows dart back and forth at amazing speeds like tiny jets and, behind an iron pipe railing, you have views in all directions. Three more plaques describe the vistas, which are all more expansive versions of the views you saw on your way up. Because you're 300 feet higher than the parking lot you can now see 13,765-foot Black Kaweah, beyond the Great Western Divide. These and other bare, pointed summits to the east are more than twice as high as the rounded, tree-topped foothills in the south and west. Beyond the foothills you can see the sometimes pink polluted haze in the San Joaquin Valley, 30 miles away and more than a mile below you.

The view of the sunset from Moro Rock may be the best in the parks. And you don't have to climb to the top to see it. Any place along the trail where you have a wide view to the west is fine. The last time we watched the sunset here the sun began its descent as a red-orange disk that silhouetted trees on the horizon and cast red light on the ridges below it. Finally, the sun became yellow-hot and the sky around it burned red like glowing hot coals.

When you're ready to return to your car, turn around, walk back down the incomparable rock and enjoy its views all over again.

---

*6,725-foot **Moro Rock** (Walk No. 28) seen from the trail to **Hanging Rock** (Walk No. 27). In the distance are the 9,180-foot Castle Rocks (left) and the south slope of the canyon of the Middle Fork of the Kaweah River.*

▶

29 Crescent Meadow

This undemanding, mostly level four-mile round trip is a grand tour of some of the most interesting features of the Giant Forest, including many huge sequoias, three wildflower-filled meadows, two primitive 19th century cabins — one built into a fallen sequoia — and a dramatic overlook on the rim of the Middle Fork canyon.

The Walk is in the southeastern part of the Giant Forest. To get to the trailhead, turn onto the Crescent Meadow Road in Giant Forest Village. Go left at the fork about a mile from the village and follow the road until it ends at a parking loop about 2.5 miles southeast of Giant Forest Village.

The Walk begins near the restrooms at the eastern end of the parking area, near the west edge of Crescent Meadow. Signs to the right of the restrooms relate some of the history of the area — including the fact that one Hale D. Tharp, who built the sequoia log home you'll see later, used Crescent, Log and Huckleberry meadows (which you'll see on the Walk) as summer pastures for his cattle until the early 19th century.

Walk through the picnic area to the left (north) of the restrooms. In about 150 feet you'll come to a sign saying that both the Chimney Tree and Huckleberry Meadow are on the path straight ahead. Then you'll immediately come to the edge of Crescent Meadow.

Keep going straight ahead along the west side of the lush, 2,000-foot-long, 200-foot-wide field. As you walk through the evergreen forest, past large sequoias and drifts of lupine, you'll have continuous views, on your right, of the meadow, which is thick with grasses, pink shooting stars, the wide, pointed leaves of corn lilies and many other Sierra wildflowers. On the other side of the narrow meadow, cinnamon-colored giant sequoias stand out sharply against the verdure.

The path gently bends to the left as it follows the curving edge of the aptly named meadow. Then the trail passes through thick ferns as it rounds the northern end of the meadow. You'll see a cluster of large sequoias to the left of the path and growths of staghorn lichen so thick on some firs that the trees look green. Here you'll also have a long view down the meadow and you'll see large clusters of tall, white-flowered cow parsnips close to the trail.

Then you'll come to a trail junction. In a few minutes you'll follow the trail to the right to Tharp's Log. Now, however, go left toward Huckleberry Meadow. In another 100 feet you'll come to another junction. Go left again.

About .2 miles from the last junction you'll see an eerie sight off to the right of the trail: the remains of a sequoia that has been severely burned. Fire has sculpted the tree into the shape of a thin, delicate, 50-foot-high black totem pole.

In another .1 mile or so you'll come to the Squatters Cabin, a plain, one-room log structure with a dirt floor, a wood-shingled roof, a fieldstone fireplace and a two-by-three-foot hole in one wall, which

served as a window. A sign explains that the cabin was built by a man in the 1880s before he discovered that the land was owned by Hale Tharp.

The short path in front of the cabin will take you quickly to the edge of Huckleberry Meadow, a charming 800-foot-long greensward that's so flat it resembles a tiny green pond. In early summer the meadow is a bouquet of blossoms, including Indian paintbrush, monkey flower and corn lilies.

Turn around here and follow the path back toward Crescent Meadow. Take a right at the first junction you come to (about .3 miles from the cabin), a left at the second and walk along the northeastern edge of Crescent Meadow. About .2 miles from the second junction you'll come to a third intersection, where the Chimney Tree will be on your left. Most of this sequoia has been burned up—it's now less than 100 feet high and it's almost completely hollowed out by fire; only its outer shell remains. Walk inside the tree, look up and you'll see the sky.

Take a right at the junction here and follow the path through large drifts of ferns and then down the east side of Crescent Meadow. You'll have constant views of the meadow on your right.

About .2 miles from the last trail junction you'll come to a sequoia that once grew by the trail but fell over. Now it stretches, like a giant log bridge, almost

---

A child is enthralled (and dwarfed by) a giant sequoia near **Crescent Meadow** *(Walk No. 29).*
◄

all the way across the meadow. Its upended roots are 15 feet high and 25 feet across.

Soon you'll come to yet another trail junction. The right fork goes back to the parking area, the left to Tharp's Log. You'll take the right fork later. Right now follow the wide, paved path to the left, past the stream on your right that trickles from Log Meadow to Crescent Meadow.

Soon you'll see the southern edge of half-mile-long Log Meadow and, a bit farther, the trail starts running along its western edge. The meadow is named after several fallen sequoias — giant logs — that stretch from one side of the narrow meadow to the other. More large sequoias, still standing, are on the other side of the meadow, which at this point is just a couple of hundred feet wide.

About .5 miles from the last junction you'll reach Tharp's Log, a fallen sequoia, hollowed out by fire, that was made into a snug "log" cabin by Hale Tharp in the mid-1800s. Tharp's Log is a more elaborate version of the log cabin in Redwood Canyon (Walk No. 14). Openings in the log (at one end, on the top and on one side) have been closed up with shingles and by a wooden door (complete with latch) that still opens and closes. The fire-scarred interior of the log has a built-in table, bench and bed. In front of the log is a split-rail corral. A sign here explains that Tharp, the "discoverer" of the Giant Forest, first visited the area in 1858 with two Indians and died at his ranch in Three Rivers in 1912, when he was 84.

Just north of the log the trail splits again. The left fork goes to the Chimney Tree, the right fork to the High Sierra Trail. Follow the trail to the right. You'll walk around the northern end of Log Meadow, which is thick with corn lilies, and you'll soon cross a wooden bridge over a small stream that runs into the meadow. Then you'll cross another tiny inlet on a stone ford and immediately come to another intersection. The path on the left is the Trail of the Sequoias, the path straight ahead goes to the High Sierra Trail.

Follow the path straight ahead, down the east side of Log Meadow. You'll pass ferns and chinquapin bushes and you'll have constant views of the meadow and the sequoia logs stretching across it.

About .5 miles from the last intersection you'll come to yet another junction, at the southeastern corner of Log Meadow. In a few minutes you'll take the right fork around the southern edge of Log Meadow. Now, however, go left and follow the trail up the evergreen-forested slope. In about .1 miles you'll come to a four-way intersection. The path on your left goes to the Trail of the Sequoias. The path in the middle and on your right are both the High Sierra Trail; the right-most trail goes back to the parking area, the middle one to Eagle View. Near the intersection are three giant sequoias: a pair of trees, both ten feet thick at the base, and another tree that's 12 feet thick at the bottom.

Take the High Sierra Trail to Eagle View. You'll immediately come to the rim of the Middle Fork canyon, from which you'll see the 9,081-foot spires of Castle Rocks, on the south side of the half-mile-deep valley. Among the manzanita bushes you'll also see the skeletons of dozens of fire-blackened trees, which were burned in the Buckeye Fire of 1988. A sign along the trail says a "carelessly discarded cigarette" caused the fire, which burned 3,100 acres, and that it took 1,200 firefighters a week to put it out—at a cost of $2.5 million.

The trail curves along the edge of the canyon and, about .2 miles from the last trail junction, brings you to Eagle View, where you'll have nearly 180-degree views up and down the canyon. The vista stretches from Moro Rock (Walk No. 28) on the right, to Castle Rocks and creased ridges on the south side of the canyon, to the pointed bare gray summits of the Great Western Divide on the left.

After you've enjoyed the view, retrace your steps to the trail junction at the southeastern edge of Log Meadow (it's the second intersection after you leave Eagle View).

Go left at the junction and follow the path along the southern edge of Log Meadow and then along the creek that runs from Log Meadow to Crescent Meadow. The banks of the tiny stream are covered with ferns, horsetails, grasses and wildflowers. On the other side of the creek you can see the paved path you walked on earlier on your way from Crescent Meadow to Log Meadow. To your left is the ridge separating Log and Crescent meadows from the Middle Fork canyon.

About .2 miles from the last trail junction the path

9,180-foot Castle Rocks and the Middle Fork of the Kaweah River, more than 4,000 feet below, seen en route to the **Paradise Creek** *and* **Middle Fork** *trails (Walks No. 32 and 33).*

▶

turns sharply to the right in front of a fallen sequoia. Then it crosses the creek on stones and immediately joins the paved path beyond it.

Follow the paved path to the left. You'll quickly see Crescent Meadow ahead of you and in just a few hundred feet you'll be at a trail junction at the meadow's eastern edge. On your right you'll see the unpaved path on which you walked along the eastern side of the meadow.

Stay on the paved path, which immediately turns left and heads through large drifts of ferns on the east side of the meadow. Right away you'll cross a usually dry wash on a plank bridge and, a few feet later, you'll cross a wooden bridge over the creek that runs from Log Meadow to Crescent Meadow.

The trail then curves to the right, along the southern end of the meadow, and soon affords you a view of almost the entire field from south to north. A sign here says the renowned conservationist John Muir called the meadow the "gem of the Sierras." Soon the paved path runs into the High Sierra Trail. The unpaved left fork of the trail goes to Eagle View; its paved right fork goes back to the parking area. Stay on the paved fork, which quickly crosses two wooden bridges over two branches of tiny Crescent Creek, the outlet of Crescent Meadow. In only a couple of hundred feet more you'll be at the parking area, just south of the restrooms, where you began the Walk.

30 Bobcat Point

This undemanding one-mile loop takes you

to two overlooks on the rim of the Middle Fork canyon, where you'll see the Great Western Divide, Castle Rocks and Moro Rock. The trail also brings you to two groups of bedrock mortars that Indians used to grind acorns, seeds and other plant parts into foodstuffs.

Like Walk No. 29 (Crescent Meadow), this Walk begins in the parking loop at the eastern end of the road to Crescent Meadow, about 2.5 miles southeast of Giant Forest Village. (If you need more exact directions to the trailhead, check the beginning of the description of Walk No. 29, on page 130.)

The Walk begins just to the right of the restrooms at the eastern end of the parking loop. Follow the High Sierra Trail, which is paved here, around the southwestern edge of Crescent Meadow, which will be on your left. You'll soon walk across two wooden bridges that cross two branches of Crescent Creek, which drains Crescent Meadow.

Less than .1 miles from the trailhead, the trail splits. The paved path goes straight ahead; the unpaved High Sierra Trail goes to the right. Take the High Sierra Trail.

In just 50 feet you'll come to another intersection. The High Sierra Trail goes straight ahead. The trail to Bobcat Point goes to the right.

Follow the righthand trail, which quickly climbs up the side of the ridge that separates Crescent and Log meadows from the Middle Fork canyon. The path curves to the left of a ledge, then runs through evergreen woods along the crest of the ridge. Through the trees on your left you'll see Castle Rocks

and other points on the steep southern slope of the canyon.

Next the trail descends slightly and, just .2 miles from the trailhead, climbs gently up to Kaweah Vista, a rock outcrop on the rim of the canyon from which you can see (partly through trees) the bare, pointed summits of the Great Western Divide, on your left; the towers and spires of Castle Rocks and the layers of sharply creased, nearly mile-high ridges beyond the southern rim of the canyon; and the rounded, 6,725-foot-high Moro Rock (Walk No. 28), on your right. You can also see deep into the canyon, whose steep sides plunge thousands of feet below you.

Walk another 200 feet, through mountain misery and manzanita bushes, and you'll come to Bobcat Point, another rock outcrop more than half a mile above the bottom of the Middle Fork canyon. Its view of the Great Western Divide is obscured by trees but you have a clear vista of Castle Rocks, directly across the canyon, and a close view of Moro Rock, about half a mile away. Beyond Moro Rock is the Ash Peaks Ridge. South of the canyon are a half-dozen layers of foothills.

When you're ready to continue, follow the trail down from Bobcat Point. In about .2 miles you'll come to ledges beside Crescent Creek. Before you cross the tiny stream, note the large pothole in the rock.

Castle Rocks seen from the **Middle Fork Trail** *(Walk No. 33).*
◀

About 100 feet from the creek you'll reach a trail junction. The path straight ahead goes to Moro Rock. The path on the right goes back to Crescent Meadow.

Take a right and in about .1 miles you'll come to a ledge that stretches across the trail. Walk about 75 feet to the left and you'll see seven cone-shaped Indian mortars carved in the bedrock. Each mortar is about seven inches deep and about eight inches across. Near the mortars are several potholes, each about a yard wide and a foot deep. According to a sign here, some people believe the potholes were made by a "prehistoric race. Others say they are the natural products of rock weathering and erosion." The mortars, on the other hand, were definitely made by Indians. As the sign explains, Indian women used them to grind acorns and other "forest products" into food.

Now go back to the trail, which immediately crosses a tiny tributary of Crescent Creek on stones and then follows Crescent Creek upstream. To the right of the creek is the long ridge you climbed on your way up to Bobcat Point.

About .3 miles from the last intersection you'll come to a metal sign indicating that more Indian mortars are on the ledge to the right of the trail. Walk about 100 feet off the trail and you'll see five mortars. The largest is nine inches deep and seven inches across at the top; the smallest is two inches deep and five inches across. You'll also find three potholes, the largest of which is a foot deep and a yard wide at the top.

Go back to the path and you'll quickly come to a

trail junction. The right fork goes to the trail to
Tharp's Log (see Walk No. 29). Take the left fork,
which runs through open, sunny woods and, about
.1 miles from the intersection, brings you back to the
parking area.

31 Crystal Cave

This undemanding 1.5-mile round trip is really two Walks in one: a .5-mile guided tour
through the most scenic marble cave in the
parks and a pleasant .5-mile nature trail that
takes you past picturesque waterfalls on your
way to and from the cavern.

Crystal Cave, in Sequoia National Park, has
become so popular that you can tour it only by
reservation. Reservations can be made, and
admission tickets purchased, only at the
Lodgepole Visitor Center.

The trail to the cave is about 4,000 feet above sea
level. Temperatures at this altitude are usually
warmer than in the Giant Forest, which is about half
a mile higher. Also, the walk back from the cave to
the parking area is almost all uphill. Because the
Walk can be uncomfortable on a hot day, you may
want to try to take it on a cool day or early in the
morning.

The cave is a 12-mile drive from the Lodgepole
Visitor Center. To reach the cavern, follow the Gen-

erals Highway south from the visitor center. After you pass through Giant Forest Village you'll have views, through the evergreen trees on your right, of the canyon of the Marble Fork of the Kaweah River. About 1.7 miles from Giant Forest Village the road passes through an impressive group of giant sequoias known as the Four Guardsmen. About 2.2 miles from the village you'll take a right onto the road to Crystal Cave and immediately start winding down to the Marble Fork canyon. About 1.7 miles from the intersection you'll cross the Marble Fork Bridge. About five miles from the bridge you'll reach the Crystal Cave parking area. You're now about 2,000 feet lower than the Giant Forest so, instead of sequoias and evergreens, you're surrounded mainly by oaks and tawny grasses. There's a public telephone here, as well as restrooms. If, incidentally, you stand at the top of the restroom steps and look to the horizon, you'll see the top of Moro Rock (Walk No. 28).

You're allowed to walk down to the cave a few minutes before your tour begins. You'll follow a wide .5-mile asphalt trail, shaded by oaks and bay laurel, down the steep canyon of Cascade Creek. (Make sure you stay on the trail and don't brush against vegetation beside it — there are a few patches of poison oak along the path.) Through the trees on your left you'll see Crystal Cave Ridge, on the opposite side of the canyon.

Indian pictographs and small bedrock mortars below them at **Potwisha** *(Walk No. 34).*
◄

About halfway down the trail you'll start hearing Cascade Creek. Then the trail curves to the right and you'll soon cross a handsome wooden footbridge over the well-named creek. A 12-foot-high cascade falls over a ledge upstream, on your right, and there's a four-foot-high cascade below it.

Then the trail switches back to the left and follows the creek through a gardenlike dell. You'll pass a narrow, 30-foot-high cascade and a series of smaller falls below it.

In another couple of hundred feet you'll be at the mouth of the cave. Across the entrance is a gray wrought iron gate designed to look like a giant spiderweb.

The 45-minute tour of the cave takes you through five different underground "rooms," the largest of which is 141 feet long, 54 feet wide and 43 feet high. An enthusiastic and knowledgeable guide will point out the cave's often amazing stalactites, stalagmites, columns, "curtains" and other formations and will explain how they were made. A 32-page pamphlet, published by the Sequoia Natural History Association (which operates the cave), also describes the cave and explains how it was formed. Illustrated with both color and black-and-white photographs, the booklet is for sale at the trailhead and at shops throughout the park.

When your tour is over, retrace your steps to the parking lot, which is 320 feet above the cave. To make the uphill walk as pleasant as possible, go slowly, pause at interesting views and take time to read the *Cascade Creek Nature Trail* pamphlet along the way. The 12-page brochure is sold in a box about 50 feet from the cave entrance and it describes the trees, flowers and shrubs you'll see along the trail.

32 Hospital Rock & Paradise Creek

This undemanding 2.6-mile excursion is a many-faceted introduction to the lovely dry oak- and-grass-covered foothills in the southern part of Sequoia National Park. At the trailhead you'll see Indian pictographs and bedrock mortars and deep rockbound pools in the Middle Fork of the Kaweah River. En route you'll have close, continuous views of the cascading Middle Fork and you'll enjoy a pleasant walk through parklike oak orchards along Paradise Creek.

The Walk begins in the large paved parking area on the Generals Highway opposite Hospital Rock, which is about six miles north of the Ash Mountain entrance of Sequoia National Park and about 10.5 miles south of Giant Forest Village. There are restrooms and a public telephone here, as well as a view of many landmarks. On the northern horizon is Hanging Rock (Walk No. 27) and Moro Rock (Walk No. 28), to the right of it. To the northeast is 11,204-foot Alta Peak. To the east are 12,205-foot Mount Stewart and other pointed peaks of the Great Western Divide. In the southeast are the 9,081-foot Castle Rocks.

On the other side of the Generals Highway is the beginning of the paved road that runs along the Middle Fork to Buckeye Flat Campground. Just to the left of the road is a big boulder. That's Hospital Rock.

Carefully cross the highway and follow the trail at the base of the rock. The handsome 50-foot path, made of ledge and stone steps, brings you beside a 15-foot-square area on the side of the rock that's covered with dull-red Indian pictographs. Some of the figures look like people. Others look like the sun. Still others are incomprehensible. According to Hale Tharp (after whom Tharp's Log [see Walk No. 29] is named), even Indians who lived here in the 19th century didn't know what the pictographs meant. They told Tharp the markings had been there as long as they could remember and they asked *him* what they represented!

On the other side of the road to Buckeye Flat Campground there are at least 34 Indian mortars in an eight-by-eighteen-foot area on top of a large boulder. The mortars are as small as one inch deep and three inches across at the top and as big as one foot deep and ten inches across. A sign here explains how Indians used these mortars to grind acorns, manzanita berries and other seeds into foodstuffs.

Now walk south along the Generals Highway, away from Hospital Rock. About 30 feet past the Indian mortars you'll see a paved path on your left. Follow the trail, which runs beneath oaks and bay laurels toward the Middle Fork. After only about 300 feet the path winds around boulders (and sometimes under them) as it descends on stone steps toward the river.

About 50 feet from the river the path splits. Go to the right and you'll immediately come to a six-foot-long, four-foot-wide fieldstone overlook from which you can see the rock-choked river. You'll have bird's-eye views of three large green pools bordered by tiny sandy beaches and by boulders the size of small houses.

Leave the overlook and keep following the path, which winds under boulders and down handsome stone steps to a beach beside the largest pool, which is 50 feet long, 20 feet wide and one to two feet deep. Children love to wade in it.

Now retrace your steps to the overlook and go another 50 feet upstream to a stony beach beside a 30-by-30-foot pool, which is deep enough for swimming. (Be careful if you take a dip. The water is cold, some rocks are slippery and the current is fast, especially in the spring.) Upstream, the river creates a white cascade as it flows into the pool. Look up, above the cascade, and you can see Moro Rock.

The green pools of the river, teeming with clear cold water, are just a few feet away from, and are a stark contrast with, the sun-parched, tawny grassland around them. The Middle Fork is a linear oasis in the dry chaparral and that fact is nowhere more obvious than here.

Now retrace your steps to the road to Buckeye Flat Campground. Start walking up the road and, about 75 feet from the Generals Highway, you'll see stone steps on your left. The seven steps will take you to— or rather *under*— Hospital Rock. The bottom of the rock is the shallow-domed ceiling of a large dirt-floored room that's about 30 feet wide, 25 feet deep and six feet high in the center, although much lower in the back and on the sides. The space is a splendid natural shelter. Hale Tharp named it Hospital Rock because an Indian medicine man treated the sick and injured here. Notice the tiny mortar (six inches deep and two inches across at the top) on a rock to the right of the entrance.

If you're short of time, you can turn around here and go back to your car. If you have time for the entire Walk, keep following the road to Buckeye Flat Campground. (Watch out for poison oak beside the road and along the trails on the rest of the Walk. Also remember the warning about ticks and rattlesnakes on page 14.) On your left, 3,000 feet above the trail, you'll see Moro and Hanging rocks. Soon, however, both landmarks disappear from view and instead you'll see the spires and towers of Castle Rocks, on the south side of the Middle Fork canyon, on your right, as well as the pools and cascades of the Middle Fork, also on your right and almost 100 feet below the road. Tawny wild oats, oaks, manzanita bushes and yuccas grow on the dry, sunny north slope of the canyon. Buckeye and redbud trees appear in the ravines and on the cooler, wetter southern slopes.

Soon the road runs along a shelf carved into the almost treeless north slope of the canyon. Now the road is a linear terrace from which you have continuous vistas of Castle Rocks and the steep golden slopes of the canyon and bird's-eye views of the cascades, green pools and wide, ledgy banks of the Middle Fork.

(You may think that you can drive to Buckeye Flat Campground and begin hiking the Paradise Creek trail from there. You can't; parking at the campground is reserved for campers. But don't feel bad: The views of the Middle Fork along the road to the campground are nowhere near as good from a car as they are on foot—you simply can't see from the inside of a car what you can see from the edge of the road.)

About .5 miles from the trailhead, the dirt road to the Middle Fork Trail (Walk No. 33) goes off on the left. Keep following the paved road, which immediately starts descending to Buckeye Flat Campground. In just a couple of hundred feet you'll come to the pleasant tree-shaded camping area (which has running water and restrooms with flush toilets; if, however, you're counting on filling your canteen here, make sure the campground is open before you leave the Hospital Rock parking area).

The road forks at a signboard at the campground entrance. Follow the paved road to the left for about 50 feet. You'll see campsite no. 28 on the right side of the road and a usually unmarked trail on the left. Follow the trail up the grassy slope, past oaks and buckeyes. Soon you'll hear, and a minute or so later you'll see, the Middle Fork on your right. As the trail starts descending to the river you'll pass several fieldstone dams and wide pools above and below them.

About .1 miles from the campground you'll cross a 40-foot-long bridge over the Middle Fork. Twenty feet below the bridge is a deep green 50-foot-wide, 150-foot-long pool and cascades above and below it.

On the other side of the river the trail forks. A faint path to the right takes you over ledges to cascades and pools in the ledgy mouth of Paradise Creek, which flows into the Middle Fork just a couple of hundred feet downstream. You might want to explore this area briefly before you come back to the intersection and take the Paradise Creek Trail, which follows a water pipe up through the oaks to the left. About 50 feet from the trail junction the path forks again. Take another left and you'll quickly come to impressive pools in the ledge along Paradise Creek. Each pool is 15 feet wide and more than 25 feet long and the creek flows in and out of them in charming white cascades.

Then the trail climbs away from the creek and switches back to the left, then to the right, as it gently ascends to a grassy grove of oaks and manzanitas that are as big as small trees. Through the trees on your left you may catch a glimpse of the Middle Fork.

Soon the trail becomes a narrow but nearly level shelf in a steep slope above a tributary of Paradise Creek. Here you'll walk through a beautiful foothills landscape: a simple, elegant composition of small blue oaks surrounded by grasses and little else: a space so clean and open that it's almost parklike.

The trail soon curves into a small ravine and crosses the tributary on stones. Then it climbs out of the ravine and crosses a slope thick with pungent mountain misery. Here you'll have views on your right (sometimes through the trees) of Moro Rock. From here it looks narrow and pointed.

Then the trail again becomes a narrow shelf on a steep, grassy slope of a canyon. Cascading Paradise Creek reappears on the right and you'll have dramatic, uninterrupted views of the steep oak- and grass-covered hillside on the other side of the stream. Behind you you'll have more views of Moro Rock and you'll also see Hanging Rock, to the left of Moro, and Bobcat Point (Walk No. 30), to the right of it.

The trail gradually descends to the creek and, about .6 miles from the campground, you'll come to its evergreen-shaded banks. This is a good spot to pause before turning around and enjoying the scenery all over again, from the other direction, as you walk back to your car.

33 Middle Fork Trail

This Walk offers often continuous views of landmarks of the Middle Fork canyon, including Moro Rock, Castle Rocks, Alta Peak and the Great Western Divide. It also takes you to a beautiful natural rock-and-water garden at Panther Creek. Depending on where you begin, the nearly level round trip is either a moderately strenuous 9.6-mile Walk or a moderate six-mile trip.

The Walk follows the route of Walk No. 32 for the first .5 miles of the road to the Buckeye Flat Campground. See page 147 for a description of Walk No. 32 as well as directions to the trailhead. Also, keep an eye out for poison oak along both the road and the trail and remember that ticks and sometimes rattlesnakes (see page 14) are found in this area.

If Buckeye Flat Campground is open (as it usually is from mid-April to mid-October) you'll be able to drive the first .5 miles of the paved road to the campground — the route of Walk No. 32 — then take a left onto the unpaved road that dead-ends at a parking area 1.8 miles from the Generals Highway. If you drive that far, your round trip will be six miles instead of 9.6 miles. On the other hand, you'll miss views of the Middle Fork that you can see only on foot. Our suggestion? If you have time and energy for the longer walk, take it. In any event we'll describe the longer version.

All of this trail is below 4,000 feet and much of it runs through unshaded chaparral. On warm, sunny days — and in the summer there are few other kinds here — that can make for hot, sweaty, annoying walking. If you can't take this Walk on a cool day, start early in the morning, when the temperature is lower than it is at midday.

After you take a left onto the dirt road to the Middle Fork Trail, you'll immediately see large cascades upstream in the Middle Fork, on your right. The road is a shelf in the steep slope of the Middle Fork canyon. It passes oaks, yuccas and acres of golden wild oats on the sun-drenched southern incline, and buckeyes and occasionally bay laurels in the wet washes on your left and right. You'll have continuous views of the south wall of the canyon and you'll soon see Castle Rocks ahead, on your right, and the Ash Peaks, down the canyon, behind you.

Then the road curves to the left and you'll see the wooden bridge over the Middle Fork, which you cross on your way to Paradise Creek (Walk No. 32).

Upstream from the bridge is a large, noisy water-fall—you can hear it from the trail—and several large pools below it.

From here until the end of the road you'll have many views of the river and continuous views of the hills on the south slope of the canyon, which have more trees than the drier, sunnier north slope.

The road curves again to the left and your view suddenly expands. Now you'll see the Great Western Divide in front of you, 11,204-foot Alta Peak on your left and Tharp's Rock in front of the peak. You'll also have uninterrupted views of the Middle Fork splashing over its ledgy bed, sometimes through 50-foot-deep gorges. The plants with the dark green resin-coated leaves growing beside the road are yerba santa.

The road ends beside a hitching post and a sign saying that Panther Creek is three miles away. Behind you you can see the top of Moro Rock.

The Middle Fork trail immediately descends into a ravine shaded by willows and alders and it crosses Moro Creek, flowing over wide ledges.

Then the trail climbs out of the ravine, curves through an old gate and emerges onto a treeless slope of the Middle Fork canyon. This area was burned in the Buckeye Fire of 1988, so you'll pass charred manzanita bushes as well as thick stands of chamise. You'll have constant views of Moro Rock to your rear and Castle Rocks to your right and you'll hear, and sometimes see, the Middle Fork below you.

Then the trail curves to the left as it gradually climbs up a side canyon. Now you'll see Bobcat Point (Walk No. 30) on top of the slope ahead of you and you'll have more views of Alta Peak and the Great Western Divide.

About 2.3 miles from Hospital Rock you'll cross another creek. Note the cattails growing in a ledge pool on your right.

Then the trail curves closer to the Middle Fork and you'll see long white cascades and green pools in the river.

About 2.8 miles from Hospital Rock you'll reach the eastern boundary of the Buckeye Fire and you'll start seeing oaks and large manzanitas again. In fact, the now sandy, nearly level trail immediately runs through a tunnel of manzanitas that are as high as 12 feet. Now the Walk offers frequent views of Moro Rock, nearly constant vistas of Castle Rocks and glimpses of the Great Western Divide.

Over the next mile the trail runs in and out of several washes—many of them pleasant places shaded by oaks, bay laurels and alders—and offers several views of the Middle Fork's pools and cascades.

About four miles from Hospital Rock the trail crosses a 50-foot-wide ledge, then switches back and forth up the slope, where you have a wide view down the Middle Fork to Moro Rock.

Then the trail runs along the edge of a steep gorge of the Middle Fork and, shortly after, quickly descends into a lovely, shady oasis watered by Panther Creek. Here large, smooth light gray ledges shape the creek into a charming natural water garden composed of long still pools linked by small cascades; the pools are surrounded by wildflowers and shaded by oaks, alders, incense-cedars and pines. A view of the gray pointed peaks of the Great Western Divide is framed by a notch in the trees.

Walk about 200 feet upstream and you'll see a 20-foot-long, 10-foot-wide cascade flowing into a striking ledge-bordered green pool that's about 12 feet long and only one or two feet wide. Below the pool, a small cascade flows into another elegant ledge-walled pool; this one is 100 feet long but in some places only two feet wide. Farther downstream—below where the trail crosses the creek—the streamlet cascades down a five-foot-long chute into a 50-foot-long pool with a lovely low undulating ledge wall. From the pool the creek glides across the ledge, plunges over the edge and cascades more than 100 feet down the cliff to the Middle Fork. Peer carefully over the edge of the cliff and you'll see long, narrow emerald-green pools in the river below.

This idyllic dell is obviously a perfect place for a long lunch before you turn around and follow the Middle Fork Trail back to your car.

34 Potwisha

This very easy .2-mile round trip takes you to three dozen Indian bedrock mortars, several Indian pictographs and a group of wide, deep, rockbound pools in the Middle Fork that are justifiably popular swimming holes.

The Walk begins near Potwisha Campground, in Sequoia National Park, about four miles north of the park's Ash Mountain entrance and about 12.5 miles south of Giant Forest Village. To reach the trailhead, take the Generals Highway to the road to the campground, which is on the north side of the road. But don't turn into the campground. Instead turn south, onto the paved road opposite the entrance to the campground. About 200 feet from the highway, turn right and drive past a recreational vehicle dumping station on your left. Then drive about 300 feet more to a parking area in front of a grove of oak trees near the Middle Fork. You'll see signs and a trash can near the trailhead, which is to the left of the parking area.

You'll walk about 100 feet before the trail splits. Go left and walk across a low, 75-foot-wide ledge. In another 50 feet you'll see your first mortar, one of at least 33 on the ledge in an area about 50 feet long and 30 feet wide. Some of the mortars are tiny — only one to three inches across at the top. Others are nine inches across and a foot deep. All are perfectly round. As the sign at Hospital Rock explains (see Walk No. 32), Indians used these bedrock mortars to grind acorns and other seeds into food.

When you reach the opposite end of the ledge, look up at the overhanging rock about 50 feet away from you. On the underside of the rock you'll see a rough drawing outlined in white. That's one of the Indian pictographs. For a closer look, walk about 50 feet past the end of the ledge, go left and climb up the rocks to the drawings. The white pictograph looks like a crude figure of a child, with a round head, a short torso and very short, round arms and legs. Smaller figures in red resemble plants and animals.

(Don't touch the drawings—the oil on your hands can harm the images.) In the ledge in front of the pictographs you can see three more tiny mortars—each one only an inch deep and less than three inches across at the top—and what appear to be the beginnings of two others.

Like the pictographs at Hospital Rock, the drawings are an enigma. Since all the pictographs are near mortars, and since mortars were used by Indian women, scholars conjecture that the drawings also may have been made by women. But no one knows why they were made.

After you've pondered the figures, climb back down to the trail and follow the now sandy path past rounded river rocks until, just a couple of hundred feet from the pictographs, you come to the Middle Fork. On your right you'll see a 50-foot-long pool, ringed by ledges and boulders, that's deep enough for swimming. Farther upstream is another ledge-walled pool, about the same size as the first but much shallower; it's perfect for wading. The river flows into the pool over a wide, smooth ledge that many swimmers use as a water slide.

Above the water slide is a 100-foot wooden suspension bridge, beneath which are still more pools. Walk across the bridge and you'll have a bird's-eye view of the pools and the water-carved ledges beside them that resemble gray sand dunes and Henry Moore sculpture. Some of the ledges contain potholes, also formed by water, that are more than a yard across. The damlike structure upstream is the concrete casing of a flume that carries water to a hydroelectric plant near the park entrance at Ash Mountain. The river flows over the flume and drops to the pool below it in an eight-foot waterfall. On the horizon upstream you can see Castle Rocks.

Like the pools at Hospital Rock, these natural swimming holes are a cool oasis in the warm, dry chaparral that surrounds them. If you take this Walk on a hot day, you'll be tempted to get wet before you retrace your steps to your car. (If you do go swimming be careful — see page 15.)

35 Paradise Ridge Trail

This moderately strenuous 2.6-mile round trip takes you to dense concentrations of giant sequoias and offers several views of the East Fork canyon and the peaks of the Great Western Divide. If you walk a total of about 3.6 miles you'll see still more giant sequoias and even more views of the East Fork canyon.

The Walk begins in the Hockett Trailhead Parking Area in the Atwell Mill Campground, on the south side of the Mineral King Highway in Sequoia

A 20-foot waterfall on the East Fork of the Kaweah River, seen from a bridge on the **Atwell-to-Hockett Trail** *(Walk No. 36).*

▶

National Park. (See page 26 for information on the road.) The parking area is about 20 miles east of Route 198, about 1.5 miles west of the Silver City Resort and about 4.2 miles west of the Mineral King ranger station.

After you've parked, walk west along the side of the Mineral King Highway. You'll pass the campground, on your left, as well as giant sequoias and relics of past logging, including 12-foot-thick sequoia logs lying on the ground and fantastic-looking 10-foot-high, 20-foot-wide sequoia stumps. In about .3 miles you'll come to the Paradise Ridge Trail, on your right, on the north side of the road.

The trail switches back and forth as it climbs steeply through a pleasant evergreen forest. You'll pass more stumps of giant sequoias and, in sunny places, you'll see manzanita bushes and carpets of pungent mountain misery.

About a quarter-mile from the highway the grade becomes less steep and the clearings more frequent and you'll begin to have views of the steep south slope of the East Fork canyon.

About .5 miles from the highway the grade becomes even gentler and the trail reenters the woods. Now you're in one of the largest *dense* concentrations of sequoias in the parks. You'll immediately see a thick cluster of giant sequoias—at least 15 in a 50-square-foot area—as well as a dozen others around the trail. You'll come to another group of sequoias a few hundred feet ahead, on your right. Then you'll cross a tiny creek surrounded by ferns and climb gently past many more giant sequoias in the next half mile.

About a mile from the highway the path comes out of the woods and into a clearing thickly grown with manzanita and ceanothus bushes. Here you have the best view on the Walk: a wide vista of the Middle Fork canyon, in front of you, and the two-mile-high peaks of the Great Western Divide, on your left.

There's another cluster of sequoias—albeit much smaller than the groups you've already walked through—in another half mile. And there are more views of the canyon along the way, though none as good as the one you're looking at now. If you feel like a longer walk and want to see more big trees, keep following the trail as it switches back and forth up Paradise Ridge. Otherwise, turn around here and follow the trail back to your car.

36 Atwell-to-Hockett Trail

This moderate two-mile round trip takes you through pleasant, open evergreen woods and down to a gorge in the East Fork of the Kaweah River. There, from a bridge over the ledge-walled stream, you'll see impressive waterfalls and large green pools.

Like Walk No. 35, this outing begins at the Hockett Trailhead Parking Area in the Atwell Mill Campground, which is on the south side of the Mineral

King Highway in Sequoia National Park. (See page 26 for information on the road.) The parking area is about 20 miles east of Route 198, about 1.5 miles west of the Silver City Resort and about 4.2 miles west of the Mineral King ranger station.

After you've parked, start walking on the unpaved road on the west side of the parking area. You'll go through the campground and pass campsites no. 18-21. Near campsite no. 11 the road forks. Follow the road to the left, toward what a sign here calls the Hockett Meadow Trail. About .2 miles from the parking area you'll reach the trailhead, which is between campsites no. 16 and 17.

The trail immediately passes remnants of late 19th-century sequoia logging: 12-foot-high, 15-foot-wide sequoia stumps and waist-high logs lying on the evergreen forest floor.

In about 100 feet the trail comes to an unmarked fork. Go left and follow the smooth, gently descending trail through pines, firs, incense-cedars and other evergreens.

In about .2 miles the trail forks again. Go right. You'll quickly see the rusty remains of the old Atwell sawmill in the small, sunny meadow on the right of the trail.

Then the trail curves to the left and starts descend-

A mule deer grazes beside the trail to **Black Wolf Falls** *(Walk No. 38) in Mineral King; 11,947-foot Vandever Peak is in the background.*
◄

ing the north slope of the East Fork canyon, an open evergreen woodland carpeted with pungent mountain misery. You'll see the opposite slope of the canyon through the trees on your right and you'll start hearing the East Fork, 800 feet below.

In about .7 miles the trail enters a small ravine and crosses a modest creek, which cascades over ledges above and below the trail. Thimbleberry bushes and a lone giant sequoia grow beside the stream.

After you cross the creek on stones, the roar of the East Fork gets louder and louder. As you approach the East Fork Bridge you'll see pools and cascades at the bottom of a gorge, on your right.

In about a mile you come to the 30-foot wooden footbridge across the river. Upstream a long, narrow waterfall, about 20 feet high and three to four feet wide, plunges between a cabin-size boulder in the middle of the river and the ledge on the streambank. There's another fall, about four feet high, below the big one, and three large, deep pools, one of which is directly under the bridge, the others farther downstream. Walled by steep ledges, the pools are about 20 to 25 feet wide and 30 feet long. Several large sequoias rise above the gorge.

The bridge is the most scenic spot on the Walk and a perfect place to stop for lunch. If you want to see a few more sequoias, cross the bridge and follow the trail for another quarter-mile or so. Otherwise, enjoy the waterfalls, turn around and follow the trail back to your car.

37 Cold Spring Nature Trail

This easy 1.6-mile round trip is an excellent introduction to Mineral King. Signs describe the trees and plants you see along the trail and you'll have views of Black Wolf Falls, the East Fork of the Kaweah and the peaks of the Great Western Divide.

The Walk begins in Cold Springs Campground, at the northern end of Mineral King valley and near the end of the Mineral King Highway, in Sequoia National Park. (See page 26 for information on the road.) The campground is about 2.6 miles east of the Silver City Resort and about 400 feet west of the Mineral King ranger station. To reach the trailhead, turn south off the Mineral King Road, into the campground. You'll immediately cross the East Fork. Take a left at the intersection on the other side of the river and in a couple of hundred feet you'll come to a small parking area by the trailhead, which is beside campsite no. six.

You'll barely start walking before you'll start seeing small metal signs attached to wooden posts. The signs identify and describe the aspens, cottonwoods, willows and other trees and plants growing around you. Read them and you'll learn, among other things, how to tell the difference between red and white firs and between Jeffrey and ponderosa pines.

At the sign explaining sagebrush, the trail splits. Take either fork and follow it until the two branches of the trail rejoin near the sign explaining Jeffrey pines, about 300 feet ahead. (Take the other branch of the trail when you walk back to the campground.)

In about a quarter-mile the nature trail signs disappear and the trail runs close to the cascading East Fork. Ahead you'll see two peaks of the Great Western Divide: the dark gray 11,509-foot Empire Mountain, on the left, and the aptly named and much lighter colored 12,393-foot Sawtooth Peak, on the right.

The trail turns away from the East Fork and runs through a grove of pole-size quaking aspens. Here you'll see the gray 11,550-foot Mineral Peak, to the right of Sawtooth Peak. On your left you'll see the steep north slopes of the East Fork canyon. Thanks in part to avalanches they're all but denuded of trees.

The trail then switches back to the right, then to the left, farther from the river. Now you'll see the slopes of the multihued 12,045-foot Rainbow Mountain, to the right of Mineral Peak. Straight ahead is Black Wolf Falls, cascading over a ledge in a crease in the steep slope below Sawtooth Peak.

The trail now runs through a meadow and you'll

Bigelow's sneezeweed blooms in White Chief Bowl on the **White Chief Trail** *(Walk No. 40) in Mineral King.*

►

have many views of the East Fork, now a few dozen feet below you, on your left.

The trail then curves to the right, following the East Fork, and you'll see the gray 12,432-foot Florence Peak, to the right of Rainbow Mountain, and the red-brown 11,588-foot Tulare Peak, to the right of Florence. To the right of Tulare Peak is Farewell Gap (Walk No. 39).

In about .8 miles the trail again curves away from the river. From here until the end of the trail, the views of the peaks are blocked by trees—which is why this is a good place to turn around and follow the path back to your car.

38 Black Wolf Falls

This .3-mile round trip takes you quickly and easily to refreshing 40-foot-high, 30-foot-wide cascades on Monarch Creek.

The Walk begins on the Mineral King Highway, about one mile past the Mineral King ranger station, .1 miles past the Sawtooth-Monarch Parking Area, about 800 feet before the road to the Mineral King pack station and about .2 miles before the end of the road. (See page 26 for information on the winding, 25-mile Mineral King Highway.) The trailhead isn't marked. Look instead for a usually dry wash, on the east side of the road, less than 100 feet south of a bridge over Monarch Creek. A row of about six large rocks stretching across the wash, close to the road, keeps people from parking in the streambed. (You'll have to cross the wash a few hundred feet ahead. If there's water in it, you may want to take this Walk on another day.) Park on the other side of the road and make sure your car is off the pavement. If you can't find a parking place along the road, leave your car in the Sawtooth-Monarch Parking Area and walk back to the trailhead.

The trail begins on the rocky north bank of the wash, about 30 feet from the road. From here you'll already see the falls, just a few hundred feet to the northeast.

You'll keep seeing the falls as the path curves through a rocky, sagebrush-covered flat. Above the falls are the jagged gray crags on the slope of 11,509-foot Empire Mountain.

In about 400 feet you'll cross the wash. (If the wash happens to have fast-flowing water in it, turn around and finish this Walk another time.) On the other side of the wash the trail turns left and follows the streambed upstream. The now-narrow trail is almost overgrown with young cottonwoods and other brush.

In about 300 feet you'll come to Monarch Creek. Stretching across the creek like a dam is a massive ochre ledge, about 30 feet wide and 40 feet high. Over this ledge the creek trickles and splatters, cascades and falls in literally hundreds of white strings of water, some of them 12 to 14 feet high. In late summer, the falls are only about 15 feet wide at the top of the ledge. But the cascades spread out as they fall, so by the time they reach the bottom of the ledge they cover the entire width of the rock. In late summer, Black Wolf isn't so much a falls—a collection of large columns of falling water — as it is a handsome natural fountain: a cooling, refreshing, mesmerizing display composed of a yellow-brown ledge decorated with glistening white water.

Look behind you and you'll see 11,120-foot Eagle Crest and 11,159-foot White Chief Peak to the south, just to the right of 11,947-foot Vandever Mountain. Left of Vandever is Farewell Gap (Walk No. 39).

After you've enjoyed this pleasant place, turn around and follow the path back to your car.

39 Farewell Gap Trail

This moderate 4.6-mile round trip takes you gently up Mineral King valley. En route you'll see four creeks — Spring, Crystal, White Chief and Franklin — cascading down the steep valley walls. You'll also have bird's-eye vistas of the East Fork and continuing views of both Farewell Canyon and Mineral King valley and the mountains around them.

The Walk begins in the Eagle-Mosquito Parking Area, which is at the very end of the Mineral King Highway, 3.9 miles past the Silver City Resort and 1.2 miles beyond the Mineral King ranger station. (See page 26 for information on the road.)

Falls on the South Fork of the Kaweah River at Ladybug Camp on the **Ladybug Trail** *(Walk No. 41).*

▶

After you've parked, start walking back on the Mineral King Road. You'll cross the East Fork of the Kaweah — here just a modest creek — and, about .1 miles from the parking area, you'll come to the unpaved road to the Mineral King pack station, on your right. Follow the road to the pack station, which is about a quarter-mile away, and walk past the corrals, on your left (keep right at all road junctions). Opposite the last corral the road narrows to a wide trail (which, incidentally, is well used by horses and mules from the pack station, so watch out for droppings). Several smaller trails leave the Farewell Gap Trail on the right; keep left at all intersections.

You're now near the bottom of Mineral King valley and you're surrounded on all sides by steep, mostly treeless slopes that rise hundreds of feet above you. You'll have views of the East Fork to your right and, on the other side of the valley, you'll see Spring Creek cascading 600 feet down the valley walls. Straight ahead you'll see 11,588-foot Tulare Peak on the left wall of the valley, 11,947-foot Vandever Peak on the right wall and, between them, 10,587-foot Farewell Gap, half a mile above you, in the south end of the valley.

The trail passes an incongruous mix of plant life: sagebrush in drier places above the floor of the valley, firs and other evergreens in moister places and willows, cottonwoods and currant bushes in wet spots near the bottom of the valley.

Soon you'll start to see the bare summit of 12,045-foot Rainbow Mountain and then the cascades of Crystal Creek, both up the slope on your left.

About .8 miles from the pack station, you'll cross

Crystal Creek on stones. The stream, which drains 10,800-foot-high Crystal Lake, spreads out wide and shallow where you cross it near the bottom of the valley. Upstream you can see the creek cascade down steep, bare ledge in hundreds of tiny white ribbons of water.

Now the path starts climbing gently away from the East Fork and up the east wall of the valley. As you climb higher you'll catch glimpses of the East Fork, which becomes smaller and whiter as you climb farther upstream and up the steepening floor of the valley. On the opposite wall of the valley you'll now see the long, thin cascades of White Chief Creek. On your left you'll have closer views of the white and rust-colored bands of rock on the slope of the well-named Rainbow Mountain. Behind you your views down Mineral King valley will be ever more sweeping.

About 1.5 miles from the pack station you'll come to Franklin Creek, which cascades for literally hundreds of feet down steep gray ledges in the valley wall. The creek is fed by the two-mile-high Franklin Lakes and creates dozens of three- and four-foot waterfalls — and some as high as 15 feet — as it tumbles down its rocky bed.

The trail crosses the creek (on stones) below a 12-foot cascade, then switches back and forth as it gently climbs up the south bank of the stream. You're now on a steep triangle of land whose two sides are the East Fork and Franklin Creek and whose apex is the junction of these streams in the bottom of the valley. The trail's odd-numbered, rightmost switchbacks are close to the East Fork; its even-numbered, leftmost switchbacks are close to Franklin Creek. At the second switchback, you'll get another view of the creek's cascades and it's even better than the view you had when you crossed the stream. You can see the top of the 12-foot cascade above the crossing, plus a pair of ten-foot cataracts; one of the cascades is six feet wide, the other is two feet wide at the top and spreads to five feet at the bottom. At the third switchback you can see the East Fork, below you and to your right. At the fourth switchback you are again near Franklin Creek and you can see 300 feet of cascades — long bands of white water falling down a V-shaped gorge. These cascades are as exciting as any falls in Mineral King. By now you also have constant views down Mineral King valley and up the slope of Timber Gap, north of the valley. At the fifth switchback, near an ancient Sierra juniper, you have another view of the East Fork and still another view at the seventh switchback. It's a pity that the trail doesn't stay close to Franklin Creek because the creek has beautiful cascades along at least a mile of its length. Higher up the trail you can see the tops of 11,120-foot Eagle Crest and 11,159-foot White Chief Peak, both rising above the north slope of Vandever Mountain about two miles to the southwest.

About .5 miles from Franklin Creek the trail straightens out and follows a narrow shelf in Farewell

Peaks of the Great Western Divide seen from the High Sierra Trail to **Bearpaw Meadow High Sierra Camp** *(Walk No. 42).*

▶

Canyon, a couple of hundred feet above the East Fork. Views of Mineral King valley disappear and instead you can see, ahead of you, the steep, braided slopes of Farewell Canyon and the notch of Farewell Gap, at the head of the canyon and about four miles farther up the trail.

This point — about 2.3 miles from the parking area — is a good place to rest before turning around and following the trail back to your car.

If, on the other hand, you want to see even more views of Farewell Canyon and Farewell Gap, keep walking as long as you want.

40 White Chief Trail

This moderately strenuous eight-mile round trip is the longest Great Walk in Mineral King and one of the longest in the parks. But it's worth the effort. It takes you up the west slope of Mineral King valley to the dramatic, 10,000-foot-high rock amphitheater known as Upper White Chief Bowl. On the way you'll see four cascading creeks, two alpine meadows and the entrance of the abandoned White Chief Mine. You'll also have views of White Chief Canyon; Mineral King valley; Empire, Rainbow and Vandever mountains; Mineral, Tulare and White Chief peaks; and Eagle Crest.

Like Walk No. 39, this outing begins in the Eagle-

Mosquito Parking Area, at the very end of the Mineral King Highway, 3.9 miles east of the Silver City Resort and 1.2 miles past the Mineral King ranger station. (See page 26 for information on the road.)

At the trailhead you'll already have a view up Mineral King valley to 10,587-foot Farewell Gap. The 11,588-foot Tulare Peak is to the left of the gap; the taller, more pointed, 11,947-foot Vandever Peak is to the right.

You'll barely start walking the nearly level trail when you'll pass the Honeymoon Cabin, a redwood-colored, board-and-batten building with a high-peaked roof, just to the left of the trail. The sign attached to the 12-by-14-foot cabin says it was built about 1930 and restored by the Mineral King Preservation Society in 1989. The cabin is usually locked but if you peek through the windows you can see some of its period furnishings.

The nearly level trail then climbs almost imperceptibly along the open west slope of the dramatic, steep-sided valley. You'll pass ferns, scattered evergreens, ceanothus and currant bushes and lots of sagebrush. You'll catch glimpses of the rushing East Fork, on your left, and you'll have continuous views of the valley's half-mile-high slopes.

In about a quarter-mile you'll cross Spring Creek on a wooden footbridge. True to its name, the creek is created by a spring a quarter of a mile up the steep slope, on your right, and cascades down to the valley floor in a long ribbon of white water.

The trail now climbs a bit more steeply up the side of the valley and you can see the Farewell Gap Trail (Walk No. 39) on the other side of the canyon,

12,045-foot Rainbow Mountain to the left of Tulare Peak, 11,509-foot Empire Mountain to your left rear and the long, flat, grassy floor of the valley.

About .1 miles from Spring Creek, a trail leaves the White Chief Trail on the left and heads down to the bottom of the valley. Stay on the White Chief Trail, which goes straight ahead, and in about .5 miles you'll go through stands of Sierra juniper. Through the evergreens you'll have your first views of Crystal Creek cascading down a long ravine on the other side of the valley. The creek is framed symmetrically by 11,550-foot Mineral Peak on the left and Rainbow Mountain on the right.

Soon you'll also see the cascades of Franklin Creek, which flows down a ravine to the right of Crystal Creek. Rainbow Mountain rises to the left of Franklin Creek and Tulare Peak looms on the right.

As you walk farther south, past manzanita, ceanothus and sagebrush, more and more of Crystal Creek will come into view. Soon you'll see more than 1,000 feet of its cascades: tiny white braided ribbons of water twisting delicately over the gray ledges that are the bones of the hillside.

In about a mile you'll come to Eagle Creek. Though usually much smaller than Spring Creek, it still supports a thick growth of willows, currants,

Fireweed blooms beside the trail from **Bearpaw Meadow High Sierra Camp** *to Hamilton Lake (Walk No. 42). The bare summits of the Great Western Divide are in the background.*
◄

dogwoods and other water-loving plant life along its banks.

The trail now climbs steeply, but briefly, up to a trail junction about .1 miles from Eagle Creek. Here the trail to Eagle and Mosquito lakes switches back to the right. Stay on the White Chief Trail, which goes straight ahead, along the steep valley wall.

The path will be nearly level for about a quarter-mile and you'll see the bare, ragged crest of Mineral Peak and the layers of white, light gray and rust-colored rock on Rainbow Mountain.

Then the trail starts climbing steeply into White Chief Canyon and you'll see bits of the upper cascades of Franklin Creek, which look like a white thread sewn in and out of the steep hillside like stitches. You'll also see the creek's lower cascades, the switchbacks of the Farewell Gap Trail to the right of the cataracts and Rainbow Mountain looming above the creek.

As you climb farther up White Chief Canyon, the trail becomes more moderate and you'll see tiny White Chief Creek in the bottom of the V-shaped canyon to your left. Farther to your left you'll see Rainbow Mountain and Tulare Peak, both handsome promontories creased with ravines and bare except for scattered evergreens and bushes on their lower slopes.

The trail then curves through a grassy, rocky clearing and along the increasingly ledgy gorge of White Chief Creek. Behind you you can now see Empire Mountain and the top of 12,393-foot Sawtooth Peak, both to the left of Mineral Peak.

Then the trail nearly levels off as it follows White

Chief Creek upstream into a flat meadow surrounded by very steep slopes.

About two miles from the trailhead you'll cross White Chief Creek on stones and walk across the east edge of the meadow. On your right you'll see rough gray rock walls and, at the bottom of the walls, steep talus slopes spilling onto the edge of the meadow. Above the walls you'll see the pointed top of 11,120-foot Eagle Crest and, left of Eagle Crest, the mesa-like 11,159-foot White Chief Peak. On your left is the lower north slope of 11,947-foot Vandever Mountain.

Now you climb up a ridge covered with lodgepole pines. On your right you'll see White Chief Creek in the meadow below and the massive gray promontories of Eagle Crest and White Chief Peak almost 2,000 feet above it.

About 2.5 miles from the trailhead you'll come out of the sparse woods and into White Chief Bowl, a .5-mile-long, .1-mile-wide meadow that slopes down to White Chief Creek, on your right. The meadow is surrounded by steep rock walls: Vandever Mountain on your left and the lower slopes of Eagle Crest and White Chief Peak on your right. Straight ahead, White Chief Creek cascades over the south wall of the bowl. The last time we were here—an early September afternoon—there were still patches of snow on Vandever Mountain as well as wide drifts of lupine, gentian, corn lilies and yampah and hosts of Bigelow's sneezeweed waving and dancing in the breeze like Wordsworth's daffodils.

The bowl is about 9,400 feet high—almost 1,600 feet higher than the trailhead—and trees have all but disappeared. You're now entering the rough, bare rock world of the High Sierra.

You'll walk about halfway across the meadow when you'll see a tiny stream trickling down the slope on your right, between Eagle Crest and White Chief Peak. That's the outlet of White Chief Lake, about 1,000 feet above the bowl. To the left of the creek is the entrance to the abandoned White Chief Mine. It's a black hole above the terrace of white marble tailings.

Near the southern end of the meadow the trail forks. The right path is the White Chief Trail, which you'll follow in a few minutes. Now, however, follow the left path, which in a few hundred feet peters out in the rocky bed of White Chief Creek near the base of the narrow, 12-foot cascades and of the almost vertical rock wall of the bowl.

From here you retrace your steps to the White Chief Trail and follow it down to White Chief Creek. Cross the tiny creek on stones, climb up to the bottom of the 50-foot-high terrace of white marble tailings at the entrance of the White Chief Mine, then scramble up the right side of the terrace to the top. It's not safe to go inside the six-foot-square entrance

---

The canyon of Hamilton Creek, seen on the walk to Hamilton Lake from **Bearpaw Meadow High Sierra Camp** *(Walk No. 42). The highest promontory on the horizon is Valhalla or Angel's Wing. Much of the rock you see is the lower slope of 12,205-foot Mount Stewart, one of the peaks of the Great Western Divide.*

▶

(although a flashlight will illuminate some of the tunnel) but the view from the terrace is great: You can see the top of Rainbow Mountain to the east-northeast and Empire Mountain and other peaks of the Great Western Divide to the north.

The mine is named after the spirit of an Indian chief. John Crabtree said he was sitting beside a campfire south of Mineral King on a summer night in 1872 when a giant Indian chief appeared to him in a vision and told him to follow him. After an all-night journey the chief brought him to the entrance of a cave—the future White Chief Mine—and told him he would find veins of pure gold inside. Alas, what gold that was found couldn't be smelted and the mine never produced even one bar of gold bullion.

When you're ready to continue, climb back down the tailings to the trail and follow it up the steep, ledgy west wall of White Chief Canyon. You'll have glimpses of the creek and the cascades to your left. Sometimes the trail is hard to follow as it climbs over ledge, so watch for ducks and cairns (as well as large, deep holes in the ledge); if you lose the path, just keep walking toward the notch farther up the canyon.

About 3.5 miles from the trailhead the trail levels off and descends again to the creek. After crossing the tiny, rocky creek on stones, the faint path climbs gently up a small, stony meadow. You're now almost 10,000 feet above sea level. The meadow grass is thin and even in late summer you'll find patches of snow in the creek bed. Behind you is a long view of Mineral King valley and, beyond it, the peaks of the Great Western Divide.

To the right of the path, at the southern end of the meadow, are the impressive remains of a stone shelter. Three walls of the 12-foot-square structure are made of rocks. The fourth wall is, economically, the vertical side of a rock outcrop.

Now the trail follows the creek, past rocks and willows, until, four miles from the trailhead, you reach Upper White Chief Bowl, a vast amphitheater surrounded on three sides by the almost vertical bare, snow-flecked rock slopes of Vandever Mountain, on the left, and White Chief Peak, on the right. In the bottom of the bowl is a tiny marsh surrounded by patches of grass and a ring of rough talus. Behind you, on the other end of Mineral King valley, is Empire Mountain. You are now 10,000 feet high—higher than you'll be on any other Great Walk in the parks—and in a cool, gray, slightly forbidding world that consists almost entirely of rock: rubble at your feet, boulders beside you and piles of talus and sweeping ledge almost all around you.

After you've contemplated this dramatic High Sierra domain, turn around and follow the trail back to your car. On your return trip you'll be walking "into" many of the views of Mineral King that you saw on your way up the valley.

41 Ladybug Trail

This moderate 3.6-mile round trip takes you along the steep north wall of the canyon of the South Fork of the Kaweah River. En route you'll have continuous views of the deep V-shaped canyon and the ridges beyond it and you'll see the dome known as Homers Nose. At Ladybug Camp you'll enjoy a .1-mile-long series of pools and cascades in the South Fork and you'll see how the campground got its name.

The Walk begins just east of the South Fork Campground, in the southwestern corner of Sequoia National Park, about 13 miles from Three Rivers. To reach the trailhead, get on Route 198 and, about .5 miles south of Three Rivers, turn east onto South Fork Drive. The increasingly narrow road runs along a shelf in the steep, dry, oak- and grass-covered slopes of the South Fork canyon. As the road follows the South Fork upstream, you'll pass occasional ranches and you'll have constant views of the V-shaped, river-carved valley.

About nine miles from Three Rivers the road becomes dirt and about .9 miles after that you'll have a view of Homers Nose, a gray, bare, 9,040-foot dome on your left. According to local legend, the dome was named after Joseph W. Homer, a rancher in Three Rivers. Homer was accompanying a government surveyor who was making a map of the area in 1872. The surveyor looked at the dome, then at the rancher and said: "Homer, that looks just like your nose." The surveyor put Homer's name beside the dome on his map and that, as they say, was that. From here the dome looks like the nose of a man lying on his back, seen from the right side of his face.

About 12 miles from Three Rivers the now-one-lane road enters Sequoia National Park. You've now climbed to about 3,500 feet and, thanks to increased rainfall at this elevation, the oaks along the road are more frequent.

In about another mile you'll enter the South Fork Campground. Follow the road until it ends at a parking area beside a corral, about .2 miles from the campground entrance. As you approach the parking area the Ladybug Trail is straight ahead.

At first the oak-shaded trail follows the south bank of the South Fork. On your left, on the other side of the rocky river, you'll see the steep north wall of the South Fork Canyon.

In just about 250 feet the trail crosses the South Fork on a wooden footbridge. Then it turns right and winds through oak woodlands on the north side of the river as it follows the South Fork upstream.

In about .5 miles you'll cross the small, rocky-bottomed Pigeon Creek and begin to have intermittent views, to your right, of the steep south slope of the South Fork canyon.

Soon you'll begin climbing gently onto the open, sunny, grassy north wall of the canyon. From here you'll have continuous views of the South Fork, below you, and the craggy, 8,000-foot-high Dennison Ridge, above the south slope of the canyon, on the southern boundary of the national park.

Three-quarters of a mile from the trailhead you'll see Putnam Creek cascading down ledges into the South Fork, on the south side of the canyon.

Then, almost a mile from the trailhead, the path curves to the left, along the canyon wall, and you'll suddenly have a dramatic, 240-degree view up the canyon and of the mountains beyond. To your left, on the horizon, you'll have another view of Homers Nose.

Now the trail briefly follows Squaw Creek upstream in a shady, ledgy ravine. Then it crosses the tiny alder-shaded creek on stones, follows it briefly downstream and quickly climbs back up to the treeless slope of the canyon.

Now the trail is nearly level as it runs along the shelf in the steep hillside. You again hear, and occasionally see, the South Fork and you have constant views of the canyon and Dennison Ridge.

Then the trail runs through woods and, about 1.8 miles from the trailhead, descends to Ladybug Camp, a cool, well-shaded flat beside the South Fork. The dell is wet enough to support evergreen trees. In fact, the pines and incense-cedars here are the first you'll see on the trail. Beneath the trees the South Fork flows through a .1-mile-long chain of wide, deep green pools linked by falls and cascades.

The pool farthest downstream is especially charming. It's surrounded by smooth, elegantly curving water-sculpted ledge. Above the pool a pair of cascades slides down two rock chutes before plunging into the smooth, green-gold water. Above the downstream edge of the pool you can see the dry oak- and grass-covered slopes of the canyon. They're a startling contrast to the large ledge pools overflowing with cold water.

Crawling silently on the rocks and ledges beside the river are countless black-dotted, liver-colored ladybugs. No one knows why so many ladybugs choose to make their home in this particular place but they've been here for as long as anyone can remember. Be careful where you step so you don't harm them.

After you've explored the cascades and pools of Ladybug Camp, follow the trail back to your car and take the South Fork Drive back to Route 198.

42 Bearpaw Meadow High Sierra Camp

On this remarkable three-day round trip you'll follow the High Sierra Trail, in Sequoia National Park, to the base of the 12,000-foot peaks of the Great Western Divide. On the first day you'll take a moderately strenuous 11.5-mile walk from Crescent Meadow to Bearpaw Meadow High Sierra Camp, where you'll spend two nights and enjoy tasty dinners and breakfasts. On the way to the camp you'll follow a nearly level trail that traverses the steep north slope of the Middle Fork canyon and you'll have often continuous views of the canyon and the snow-flecked peaks of the Great Western Divide. On the second day you'll take a moderately strenuous eight-mile round trip to Hamilton Lake. En route you'll enjoy dramatic cliffside views of the steep canyons of the Middle Fork and Lone Pine and Hamilton creeks.

On the third day you'll retrace your steps on the
High Sierra Trail to Crescent Meadow.

You need reservations to stay at the High Sierra
Camp. Unfortunately, the camp is so popular that
it's usually booked for the entire season (about mid-
June to mid-September) just a few *hours* after its
reservation desk starts accepting reservations at 7
a.m. on the preceding January 2. However, many
people cancel their reservations. So if you arrive in
the parks without one, call the reservation desk every
day at 209-561-3314 and ask if they've gotten a can-
cellation. If you're flexible about when you can go,
chances are good that you can get a last-minute
reservation.

And if you can get only one night's reservation
instead of two, you can turn a three-day excursion
into a two-day one simply by walking only the first
and third day's itinerary.

The facilities at Bearpaw are rustic but perfectly
comfortable. You sleep in a two-person tent set on a
wooden platform. The canvas tent is furnished with
twin metal beds, two canvas chairs, shelves, a kerosene lamp, a mirror and a metal pitcher and wash-
basin. The bed is made up with fresh linen, three
blankets and a comforter. Soap, towels and a wash-

*The quarter-mile-long Hamilton Lake fills an 8,300-foot-
high bowl in the Great Western Divide, four miles from*
Bearpaw Meadow High Sierra Camp *(Walk No.
42).*
◄

cloth are provided and hot showers are available near the dining tent. All you need to bring are what you would bring on any long day hike, plus some personal toilet articles, some changes of socks and other clothes and perhaps something warm to sleep in.

Served family style, meals are tasty and portions are virtually unlimited. A typical meal: salad, roast turkey breast with gravy and cranberry sauce, mashed potatoes, green beans, homemade bread and delicious homemade pumpkin pie. Wine is available for a small extra charge. Breakfast is typically scrambled eggs, pancakes and muffins or other pastries. Coffee, tea and cocoa are served with all meals. Bag lunches are sold separately and usually include a large sandwich on homemade bread — your choice of ham, cheese, peanut butter or whatever meat is left over from the previous day's dinner — a piece of fresh fruit, raisins, nuts, fruit juice and homemade cookies, brownies or other home-baked sweets.

Bearpaw is known for its informality. Partly that's a result of scale: it has room for just 12 guests and its staff consists of just two people. All guests eat at one long table a few feet from the kitchen. Everyone gets to know — and, it seems, almost always likes — everyone else pretty quickly. But Bearpaw's easy ways are due mainly to its accommodating staff. When one guest asked for applesauce with his roast pork, the waiter informed him there was no applesauce but brought him some canned apples instead. When another guest said she was hungry at bedtime she was offered some cocoa and brownies.

I also remember how much I liked shaving at an

outdoor sink that had a wide view of the south slope of the Middle Fork canyon.

Although most of the first day's walk is nearly level, the trip is considered moderately strenuous for two reasons: The trail is relatively long and it's often in the open. That combination can make for hot, fatiguing walking, especially on warm days. We therefore suggest you start early in the morning—by 8 at the very latest. That way you'll be able to go at a moderate pace, savor the incomparable views and still make it to the camp in time for dinner. Also, if you start early you'll do much of your walking in the cool early part of the day.

Like Walks No. 29 and 30 (Crescent Meadow and Bobcat Point) this excursion begins at the parking loop at the eastern end of the road to Crescent Meadow, about 2.5 miles southeast of Giant Forest Village. Like Walk No. 30, this trip begins just to the right of the restrooms at the eastern end of the parking loop.

Follow the High Sierra Trail (which is paved here) around the south end of Crescent Meadow. Less than .1 miles from the trailhead, the path forks. The paved path goes straight ahead. The High Sierra Trail (now unpaved) goes to the right.

In another 50 feet there's another trail junction. The path to Bobcat Point goes to the right. The wide, smooth High Sierra Trail goes straight ahead and begins a very gradual climb, through an open evergreen forest, to the crest of the ridge that separates Crescent and Log meadows, on your left, from the Middle Fork canyon, on your right. You'll catch glimpses of Log Meadow through the trees.

In about .5 miles you'll come to a junction of three trails at the top of the ridge. If you've already taken the Crescent Meadow Walk (No. 29) this place will be familiar. The left-most trail goes to Log Meadow, the middle path is the Trail of the Sequoias and the right-most path is the High Sierra Trail. Stay on the High Sierra Trail, which goes straight ahead. Near the intersection is a pair of giant sequoias—each one ten feet thick at the base—and another sequoia that's 12 feet wide at the bottom.

Now the High Sierra Trail follows the rim of the Middle Fork Canyon (and retraces part of the route of Walk No. 29). On the other side of the half-mile-deep valley you'll see the towers and spires of 9,081-foot Castle Rocks. You'll also see the fire-blackened skeletons of dozens of trees that were burned in the Buckeye Fire of 1988.

In about .8 miles you'll come to Eagle View, where the panorama expands to 180 degrees. Your view now stretches down the canyon to Moro Rock (Walk No. 28), on your right, to Castle Rocks and the creased ridges on the other side of the canyon and to the pointed, bare granite summits of the Great Western Divide, on your left.

The views of Castle Rocks and the Great Western Divide continue as the nearly level trail follows a shelf in the steep north wall of the canyon. The pleasant path takes you beside boulders, along the base of cliffs, through dry washes and past manzanita bushes and wide carpets of pungent mountain misery, a low ground cover whose rows of tiny leaves make it look like miniature ferns.

The trail becomes shadier as it passes through oak

and pine woods. Then it switches gently back and forth up the slope and passes through a thicker, evergreen forest. Through openings in the trees you'll have occasional views of the Great Western Divide.

In about 2.5 miles the High Sierra Trail passes the trail to the Wolverton Corrals, on the left, then gradually descends into the small canyon of Panther Creek. Ahead of you, through the trees, you'll see the creek's cascades. Then, about three miles from the trailhead, you'll cross the creek, which spills over steep ledges above and below the trail. Ferns grow in the cool, shady ravine and, if you look downstream, you'll see Castle Rocks.

About .6 miles farther you'll enter another ravine and cross another branch of Panther Creek, which slides and trickles over ledges above and below the trail. The streambed is a natural garden of Indian paintbrush and other wildflowers. You can see pinnacles below Panther Gap (Walk No. 22), to the left of the trail, and you'll have another view of Castle Rocks and the slopes of the Middle Fork canyon, on your right.

Next the trail crosses several tiny streams and passes in and out of shady woods, sunny clearings and moist ravines as it gradually climbs up the ridge of Sevenmile Hill. Near the top of the ridge, the trail curves to the left and passes a five-foot-square boulder on the right of the trail. Here, through the trees, you have another view of the Great Western Divide.

Now, about four miles from Crescent Meadow, the trail gradually comes out of the woods and onto a shelf carved into the nearly vertical rock wall of the canyon. The next three miles of the High Sierra Trail is perhaps the best walking in the parks. For here the trail is a corniche, a long, curving platform cut into the edge of the canyon, an almost level linear terrace from which you have uninterrupted, panoramic, clifftop vistas of the canyon, Castle Rocks and the Great Western Divide.

Soon you'll also have your first view of 7,875-foot-high Sugarbowl Dome, three miles ahead of you, on the north slope of the canyon.

Then, straight ahead, you'll see the gray granite walls of the east side of the Mehrten Creek ravine. Next you'll hear the creek. Then you'll see the stream trickling and cascading down wide, flat granite ledges.

About 5.6 miles from the trailhead you'll cross Mehrten Creek on stones. The crossing is a special place: It's a cool, evergreen-shaded oasis in the bare, sunny rock slope; it has a fine view of Castle Rocks; and it's about halfway to the High Sierra Camp— three reasons why it's probably the most popular lunch spot on the trail. (Mehrten Creek, incidentally, runs out of Mehrten Meadow, the destination of Walk No. 22.)

In another 50 feet you'll cross another branch of the creek flowing in a long crack in the ledge.

Then you'll walk over the ledge, out of the ravine and back onto the corniche at the edge of the Middle Fork canyon. As you round the edge of the slope you'll have an eye-popping view up and down the canyon—all the way from the Great Western Divide on the left to Moro Rock on the right.

About 6.3 miles from Crescent Meadow the Sevenmile Hill Trail enters the High Sierra Trail on the left. From the trailhead to this junction the High Sierra Trail has climbed imperceptibly, only about 100 feet per mile. From here to the bottom of Buck Canyon, about 3.7 miles away, the trail will descend at about the same rate. It will run into shady evergreen woods, where you'll have only occasional views through the trees; into ravines where tiny creeks trickle over ledges and lush wildflower gardens bloom; and back onto the corniche cut into the steep, bare ledge, where you'll have continual views up and down the canyon.

As you get closer to the Great Western Divide, you'll begin to see snow patches, even in August, on the steep, creased peaks. You'll also have more views of Sugarbowl Dome and, as the trail curves to the left around the clifflike canyon wall, you'll have your first view of Little Blue Dome. This 7,325-foot-high dome — which is really dark gray — is to the left of Sugarbowl Dome and higher up the slope of the canyon.

About seven miles from the trailhead you'll enter a lush, steep ravine. Then, on stones, you'll cross the first of three branches of Buck Creek, trickling and cascading several hundred feet above and below the trail.

The trail then reenters evergreen woods and, through openings in the trees, you'll have more views of Sugarbowl and Little Blue domes and the Great Western Divide.

About 8.5 miles from Crescent Meadow you'll cross another branch of Buck Creek on stones. Look upstream and you'll see the small creek tumbling down boulders and steep ledges. You may also notice the brown metal food locker under the trees on the west side of the creek. Campers leave their food in these boxes to keep it away from bears.

The trail briefly follows the steep, gravelly banks of the creek downstream, then crosses a tiny stream running over ledge and again enters evergreen woods. Views of the Great Western Divide are now blocked by Sugarbowl Dome, which is part of the steep ridge on the east side of Buck Canyon.

About 9.5 miles from the trailhead the now stony path starts descending the open, sunny west slope of Buck Canyon and in another half-mile crosses Buck Creek on a concrete bridge. The creek bed is a massive jumble of rocks and its steep, bare, sandy banks are badly eroded—evidence that the creek must be a torrent in springtime.

The trail briefly follows the creek upstream, then switches back to the right and climbs up the ridge on the wooded slope of the canyon. Through the trees on your right you'll see the canyon's steep, clifflike, evergreen-festooned walls. In the distance you'll see Little Blue Dome and even Moro Rock.

Then the trail switches back to the left, around the southern edge of the ridge, and climbs more gently up the bottom of a wide, shaded ravine.

The trail then switches back to the right and climbs another ridge. Through the evergreens on your right you'll have more views of Buck Canyon.

Then the path switches back to the left and gradually levels out before crossing the top of the ridge. Here, about 11 miles from the trailhead, you'll come to a trail junction. The right fork goes to Bearpaw Meadow Campground. Take the left fork, which gradually descends, through open woods, to Bearpaw Meadow High Sierra Camp. Straight ahead you'll have another view of the Great Western Divide.

In a couple of hundred feet the trail to Tamarack Lake enters the High Sierra Trail on the left and, 11.3 miles from Crescent Meadow, you'll see the white tents of the High Sierra Camp.

Walk around to the porch of the dining tent and you'll see the best view of the day—in fact, one of the best views in the entire Sierra Nevada. Directly ahead of you, rising more than 6,000 feet up from the Middle Fork canyon, is the Great Western Divide, a stunning wall of bare snow-flecked peaks and even higher mountains behind it. A sign identifies the summits: Black Kaweah, the tallest at 13,765 feet; Queen Kaweah, 13,360 feet—both behind the Great Western Divide—and five peaks *on* the Divide—Eagle Scout, Diamond Dog, Lippincott, Eisen and Stewart—that are all more than 12,000 feet high. Take off your pack and enjoy what is perhaps the greatest pleasure of Bearpaw: taking a seat in a canvas chair, having a glass of lemonade or cup of cocoa (free) and pondering the remarkable, rare grandeur in front of you.

* * *

The round trip to the Hamilton Lakes offers continuous cliffside vistas of the steep canyons of the Middle Fork and Hamilton and Lone Pine creeks. You'll also enjoy dramatic views of the rockbound Hamilton Lakes, you'll see several "hanging gardens" (see below) and many cascades and you'll have close views of Angel's Wing (also known as Valhalla) and several peaks of the Great Western Divide.

The Walk begins on the north side of the dining tent. The smooth path runs through evergreen woods and small, wildflower-filled meadows as it gradually descends to the edge of the Middle Fork canyon. En route you'll have close views of the Great Western Divide and your vistas of the Middle Fork canyon will extend all the way from the canyon of Lone Pine Creek, to the north, to the canyon of Eagle Scout Creek, to the south.

In about .5 miles you'll reach the rim of the Middle Fork canyon. Now the trail becomes a corniche that winds dramatically along the edge of the nearly vertical canyon walls. As you pass steep ledges and boulders on your left you'll have continuing clifftop views of the Kings River, hundreds of feet below. Across the canyon you'll see the awesome canyon of Hamilton Creek, which drains Hamilton Lake. You'll have close views of the slopes of 12,205-foot Mt. Stewart, which form the north wall of the canyon; the base of 12,040-foot Eagle Scout Peak, which forms the south wall; and other mountains of the Great Western Divide. The trail also crosses several creeks cascading down the steep canyon walls. Growing in the almost vertical beds of these tiny streams are lush "hanging gardens" of ferns and colorful wildflowers.

In a bit over a mile from the trailhead you'll be above the junction of Hamilton and Lone Pine creeks — the beginning of the Middle Fork of the Kaweah — almost 500 feet below the trail. Then the path runs parallel to Lone Pine Creek as it gradually descends to the large, cascading, rocky-bottomed stream in the bottom of a steep gorge.

After about 1.5 miles the trail crosses Lone Pine Creek on a concrete bridge. When you reach the eastern end of the bridge, look upstream. You'll see a long, slender waterfall pouring through a narrow gap in the ledge.

The trail now follows the creek briefly downstream, then turns away from it and, in 1.6 miles, comes to an intersection. Tamarack Lake is to the left. Go straight ahead and follow the stony Hamilton Lake trail, which soon climbs, in long switchbacks, up the steep, bare, rocky slope of the Lone Pine Creek canyon. From here you'll see the waterfall up Lone Pine Creek, as well as the ledgy gorge of the Lone Pine Creek canyon, the forested bottom of the Middle Fork canyon and the Great Western Divide.

After climbing for less than .5 miles, the trail levels out, curves to the left along the nearly vertical slope and enters the canyon of Hamilton Creek. The trail is again a corniche cut into a shelf in the clifflike canyon wall and you'll have continuous, awesome views in three directions. Ahead and to the right are the half-mile-high walls of the canyon, the steep slopes of Eagle Scout Peak sweeping up from the canyon and, beyond them, the high, rough, massive, intimidating summits of the Great Western Divide. Five hundred feet below you is Hamilton Creek. To your rear you can see Lone Pine and Middle Fork canyons and the trail where you just walked etched into the nearly vertical canyon walls. Here the world is made entirely of peaks and cliffs—the one you're walking on and the ones all around you.

The trail gradually switches back and forth down the side of the canyon. At the head of the gorge you'll see the butte-shaped promontory known as both An-gel's Wing and Valhalla, the mythical hall of the Norse god Odin. To the right of the promontory is the white ribbon of Hamilton Creek flowing over the canyon headwall.

Then the trail again follows a shelf in the canyon wall and soon crosses a tiny creek trickling down a cleft in the cliff. The path then climbs toward the cascade of Hamilton Creek sliding over the smooth, brown-stained ledge ahead of you.

The path crosses the creek on a nearly level rock terrace above the cascade. Then the trail becomes slightly rougher as it switches back and forth up the steep slope on the south bank of the creek. As you climb the stony trail and peer through the willows along the creek, you'll glimpse more cascades, in-cluding a 30-foot-high fall tumbling down the steep, rocky notch of the canyon. On your left you'll see both Angel's Wing and the corniche on the side of the canyon where you just walked.

The trail then straightens out and briefly follows the cascading willow-choked creek before coming to tiny Lower Hamilton Lake. Then the trail quickly climbs above the lake, giving you bird's-eye views of the shallow green tarn. The last time we were there it was nearly bisected by a long sandbar extending from its western shore.

Now the trail climbs briefly beside cascading Hamilton Creek. When the path levels off you'll see Upper Hamilton Lake through the pine trees.

Then the trail descends gently and, less than a quarter-mile from Lower Hamilton Lake, reaches the ledgy west shore of Upper Hamilton Lake.

The quarter-mile-long upper lake lies at the bottom of a steep glacier-carved amphitheater. Streams cascade and trickle down the nearly bare, half-mile-high walls of the bowl in long, crinkly white ribbons. Here, in this 8,300-foot-high mountain fastness, you are far above the ordinary, soft, organic world of soil, flowers and trees. You're now in an awesome, hard and slightly forbidding place that seems to be made of nothing but rough rock and water. It's a place perhaps more fit for Norse gods than tender mortals but it's an impressive setting for a long, leisurely lunch before you follow the trail back to the High Sierra Camp and enjoy the continuous, dramatic vistas again from another perspective.

Incidentally, the stony trail from Lower Hamilton Lake to the crossing of Hamilton Creek can be slippery when you're going downhill, so take your time and watch your step.

To Our Readers:

Please help us stay current. If you discover that anything described in this guide has changed, let us know so we can make corrections in future editions. Please write to: Great Walks, Box 410, Goffstown, NH 03045. Thank you.

Great Walks of Yosemite National Park

The incomparable Yosemite National Park is just a few hours' drive from Sequoia & Kings Canyon and it has 28 Great Walks. Fourteen Walks offer views of major waterfalls. Eleven take you along the shores of beautiful lakes. Six provide stunning views of Yosemite Valley and nearby landmarks from overlooks on or near the valley rim. Two Walks are through groves of giant sequoias. Four offer views of the domes and other rock sculpture of the Tenaya Lake basin; four others show you Tuolumne Meadows and the mountains and domes around it. Six Walks feature close views of the snowcapped peaks of the Sierra Crest.

All 28 Walks are carefully described in *Great Walks of Yosemite National Park.* Like all Great Walks guides, *Yosemite* is pocket size and lavishly illustrated with beautiful full-color photographs.

To order your copy send $8.95 plus $1.50 for shipping and handling to: Great Walks, PO Box 410, Goffstown, NH 03045. Your guide will be sent to you immediately.

If you liked Sequoia & Kings Canyon, you'll *love* Yosemite! And no guide will help you enjoy it more than *Great Walks of Yosemite National Park.*

Other Great Walks Guides Already Published Include:

▶ *Great Walks of Acadia National Park & Mount Desert Island:* 32 Walks on Maine's Mount Desert Island, known for its low, ledge-topped mountains and rock-bound, island-dotted seacoast.

▶ *Great Walks of Southern Arizona:* six Walks in the fascinating mountains, canyons and basins of the Sonoran Desert near Phoenix and Tucson.

▶ *Great Walks of Big Bend National Park:* six Walks in the Chisos Mountains, the deep canyons of the Rio Grande and the Chihuahuan Desert, all at the "big bend" of the Rio Grande in southwest Texas.

▶ *Great Walks of the Great Smokies:* 20 Walks to historic sites, impressive waterfalls and cascades, and exciting mountain vistas in Great Smoky Mountains National Park, which straddles the Appalachian Crest in Tennessee and North Carolina.

The *Great Smokies* guide costs $5.95; the *Southern Arizona* and *Big Bend* guides are $3.95 each; the *Acadia* and *Yosemite* guides are $8.95 each.

You can buy Great Walks guides in bookstores or you can order them directly from the publisher by sending a check or money order for the price of each guide you want, plus $1.50 for mailing and handling the order, to: Great Walks, Box 410, Goffstown, NH 03045.

You can also receive more information on the series by sending $1 (refundable with your first order) to Great Walks at the address above.

Own an Original Oktavec Photograph

You can own an original print of any Eileen Oktavec photograph in this guide.

At your request, we will custom make a high-quality, 9¼-by-14-inch color print of your favorite Sequoia & Kings Canyon photograph(s). The print will be hand labeled, numbered and signed by the photographer. (Because the photograph will be printed on high-gloss paper, and much larger than the photograph in the guide, it will be even clearer and more detailed.)

An original Oktavec photographic print is so many things: a treasured memento of Sequoia & Kings Canyon, a masterful depiction of its world-famous scenic treasures, a valuable addition to your collection of visual art and, of course, an excellent gift.

To order, simply tell us what print(s) you would like and enclose a check for $76 for each print, plus $4 for shipping and handling any order. Send your order to Great Walks, PO Box 410, Goffstown, NH 03045. Allow 2-3 weeks for delivery.